FOR BABY

Reinforce the personal vibrations for a more positive future

STEVEN JOHN

W. Foulsham & Co. Ltd.

London ● New York ● Toronto ● Cape Town ● Sydney

Use the ancient power of numerology to help choose a
name for your baby and improve its chances of
success in our ever competitive world.

Your name can improve your destiny or be that
stumbling block that always holds you back. Check
your name and see if it matches your birth numbers.

Steven John

125455   1685
22/4   20/2

Clairvoyant Extraordinaire

Author of Your Lucky Number

W. Foulsham & Company Limited
Yeovil Road, Slough, Berkshire, SL1 4JH

ISBN 0-572-01430-9

Printed at St Edmundsbury Press,
Bury St Edmunds.

CONTENTS

INTRODUCTION

We all have a name; some of us like it, others of us wish we could change it. And yet, what is a name?

A name is a means by which we introduce ourselves to people. It is the first thing that others have to judge us on, though they may react to us differently on further acquaintance.

In school, Cedric may have been teased because of his name. That name, to aggressive, unruly people is likely to be regarded as 'cissy' or 'softy', whereas more genteel people may associate it with grace and sensitivity. In fact that person may demonstrate quite different qualities. What is most important to understand, however, is that a name interacts with our birth vibration numerologically, and may strengthen it. In short, our name has an influence on the circumstances in our lives and the way we may meet them.

Think of the name Steven with a 'v'. It vibrates to the number 22/4, which means to be brought before the public. This does not mean that all Stevens with a 'v' will work in front of the public; that must stem from the inner, or stronger birth number. The Steven merely strengthens the birth number in some cases, or opposes it in others. Some Stevens are basically shy and yet the name vibration forces them to project a side of themselves that is not really there, which can only lead to some degree of unhappiness in their inner selves.

For example, a Steven born on 9.1.57 is a 32/5 by birth. The added vibration of 22/4 totals 54/9 which encompasses both the birth and name number which will express themselves through the 9. Therefore a Steven with this date of birth will react aggressively to life and its obstacles, in tune with the communicative ability of the 32/5.

On the other hand, a Steven born on 29.1.57, has a birth vibration of 52/7; with the added name vibration of 22/4 this becomes a 74/2. This Steven is much shyer and requires partners for help and support, not in tune with the desires of the birth vibration of the 52/7.

So, as we have shown, a name helps us to project our birth vibrations, or can be an opposing force that holds us back. Therefore, in order to give our children the best possible chances in life, we should carefully choose a name in tune with the date of birth.

A name may only be a lesser force to the birth number, but it can be that extra force that determines whether or not we are successful in life, and it definitely improves our chances of being recognised for what we are, or can do so much sooner.

HOW TO CALCULATE BIRTH NUMBERS

The process is an easy one and is laid out in four simple steps.

Step one: Add day number to month number as a whole
e.g. 5th Feb = 5 + 2 = 7
15th Feb = 15 + 2 = 17

Step Two: Add Year together
e.g. 1985 = 1 + 9 + 8 + 5 = 23
1957 = 1 + 9 + 5 + 7 = 22

Step Three: Add Totals together
e.g. 5th Feb 1985 = 5 + 2 = 7
1 + 9 + 8 + 5 = 23
7 + 23 = 30

Step Four: Add first digit to second
e.g. 3 + 0 = 3

Answer: Born 5.2.85 Birth Number = 30/3
This birth number is 30 over 3

Another example: Born 26th June 1976

$$26 + 6 = 32 \qquad 1 + 9 + 7 + 6 = 23$$
$$32 + 23 = 55$$
$$5 + 5 = 10$$
$$1 + 0 = 1$$

Answer: 55/1

Now that we have ascertained the birth vibration we need simply to refer to the compatible numbers chart (p. 9) and seek names that are in tune with it. There are three choices to be made:

    1. to strengthen the birth number
    2. to force a development number
    3. to give a safe number

These are explained in the following chapter.

HOW YOU CAN HELP YOUR BABY

Your choice of directional numbers should be based on the following considerations.

1 Your choice of name number can strengthen the birth vibration by having the same base or final number as the birth number.
E.g.: born 9.1.57 = 32/5
Name: Donald = $4 + 6 + 5 + 1 + 3 + 4 = 23/5$
Both reduce to a 5 and strengthen vitality of the birth number.

2 Your choice of name number can cause development by being the next base number up which gives a foothold on your child's future.
E.g.: born 9.1.57 = 32/5
Name: Patrick = $7 + 1 + 2 + 9 + 9 + 3 + 2 = 33/6$
This number must always be one number higher than the present incarnation, i.e. 32/5, next number 33/6.
A 24/6 is not the next number higher.

3 Your third choice is to give stability and security. This is calculated by finding a name number exactly the same as the birth number.
E.g.: born 9.1.57 = 32/5
Name: Denver = 4 + 5 + 5 + 4 + 5 + 9 = 32/5

So now you must choose with care, as the name you give your child has the power to help, hinder or develop that which you love most.

Points to note:

1 All names listed are in order of their base number, e.g. 26/8 is under 8.

2 If a name you require is not listed, or you wish to make up your own, the alphabetical vibrations are as follows:
A 1, B 2, C 3, D 4, E 5, F 6, G 7, H 8, I 9, J 1, K 2, L 3, M 4, N 5, O 6, P 7, Q 8, R 9, S 1, T 2, U 3, V 4, W 5, X 6, Y 7, Z 8

3 The third point to be made here is that in this system of numerology the surname is not used, only forenames. The reason for this is that in centuries gone by, the social order of things left sons and daughters with little choice of vocation or employment. You simply learned your trade from your mother or father and continued in that occupation. Nowadays, this is not so; few people follow the vocation or occupation of their parents and become free agents while in their teens.

It is, therefore, a recommendation that you omit the surname from the calculation of your total vibration, as a surname is only of use in a formal introduction, and merely shows what our forefathers were.

On making social contacts, when we are asked our names, society no longer demands titles, airs or graces. You would not introduce yourself to a girl as Benjamin John Franklin, it would be Ben, or Benjamin. And the name we are most commonly known by is the one by which we introduce ourselves.

Radical though this may seem to some it is after a great deal of research and time spent in professional analyses that I make this recommendation. It is the name you are known by that helps to rectify your birth vibrations, so study carefully before you choose.

FIRST VOWELS IN NAMES

The first vowel in any name adds that quality as an initial contact or strength of the individual. Although not of great strength in the overall vibration it can be an indication of our conscious ability to make decisions in life.

The general vowel meanings are as follows:

A   Ambition, leadership, assertion

E   Travel, communication, pleasure

I   Intuition, sensitivity, emotion

O   Study, concentration, completion

U   Protection, inner strength

A deep study of vowels has not been included in this book as there is the possibility that the overall combination of variants in a name can be clouded; they are merely a facet of the overall personality.

NUMBER PATTERNS

A name is a series of numerical vibrations and, although the end result number may be the same, the combination numbers are of a different order.

Thus: HARRIS

> 819991 = 37/1
>
> HILARY
>
> 893197 = 37/1

Both start with an 8, but from then on alter in how they go about achieving their own specific vibration. So when choosing a name, try to select one with more combinations of the number qualities you wish to add.

E.g.: born 12.3.65 = 15 + 21 = 36/9

The 9 is in tune with 3, 6 or other 9s. A development number one higher, 37/1 with more of these numbers, helps to achieve greater success. Harris has 3×9, Hilary has 2×9, 1×3. Thus, if more energy is required, the Harris 9s are suited, but if a little thought and luck are needed, Hilary is better.

Remember, 1, 4 and 8 are compatible

> 3, 6 and 9 are compatible
>
> 2, 5 and 7 are compatible

A safe name for a 36/9 born on 12.3.65 would be one with strong 3s, 6s and 9s in the name of that number.

E.g.: boy, Vivien

> 494955 = 36 (2×9 in the name)
>
> + base number 36/9
>
> girl, Tiffany
>
> 2966157 = 36 ($1 \times 9 + 2 \times 6$ in the name)
>
> + base number 36/9

BASIC NUMBER VALUES

No.	Word	Planet	Colour
1	To lead, ambition, zeal	Sun	White
2	To feel, intuition, partnership	Moon	Silver
3	To think, communicate, imagine	Jupiter	Mauve
4	To build, realise, do	Uranus	Orange
5	To communicate, travel, adventure	Mercury	Burgundy
6	To love, create, express	Venus	Green
7	Intuition, spirituality, security	Neptune	Blue
8	To work, consolidate, mine	Saturn	Black
9	To energise, protect, do, impatient	Mars	Red
11	Spiritual rebirth, love, harmony	Moon/ Neptune	Silver/ Blue
22	Public career, public service	Uranus/ Mars	Orange/ Red
33	End of conflict, Christ, saviour higher self	Venus/ Jupiter	Green/ Mauve

So combinations of numbers to make totals can add these qualities to the birth number example.

E.g.: John
   1685 = 20/2

Overall 2 to feel

Lesser parts not in final number but parts of:

1 Sun to lead and achieve

6 Venus to relax and unwind

8 Saturn to consolidate

5 Mercury to communicate

Remember the final number is the strongest, but lesser numbers can give relief and assist that end vibration.

SUMMARY OF THE ALPHABET

Too deep an analysis would be confusing to all but initiates of metaphysical mathematics. However, I have included a basic interpretation of the number values of the alphabet to show how different names achieve their vibrations.

A	1st vowel	To lead, independence, initiative, creation.
B	2nd letter	To develop the mixing of male and female, to share.
C	3rd letter	To begin to wonder why, to experience, philosophise.
D	4th letter	To consolidate and build upon experience.
E	2nd vowel	To express, communicate and relate your experience.
F	6th letter	To consolidate, rest and share with others.
G	7th letter	To seek that which is beyond the material world.
H	8th letter	To begin to use abilities, power, business.
I	3rd vowel	To be absolute, resolute, the law, society.
J	10th letter	To aspire, to join with and fulfil dreams.
K	11th letter	To absorb the soul into the body, to realise oneself.
L	12th letter	To instigate work and create opportunities.
M	13th letter	To bring the spirit down on the material plane.
N	14th letter	To imagine, dream and reincarnate past selves.
O	4th vowel	To apply the higher mind to study.
P	16th letter	To achieve and establish the idea into reality.
Q	17th letter	To bring material security to oneself.
R	18th letter	To seek the next rung on your karmic ladder.
S	19th letter	To start your dreams and see different views.

T	20th letter	To expand, share, help and assist your fellow man.
U	5th vowel	To assess your situation, to achieve success.
V	22nd letter	To work for the betterment of all, not self.
W	23rd letter	To be free, to relax, and enjoy with all.
X	24th letter	To build a family or express sexuality.
Y	25th letter	To free the imagination and spirit for fuller growth.
Z	26th letter	To hope and dream, and share all you have seen.

All that is left for you to do now is find a name that suits your vibration, assess its qualities from the above list and ensure your baby an easier path through life's turmoil.

E.g.: born 9.1.57 = 32/5   Name, Steven John Culbert
$$125455 \quad 1685$$
$$22 \qquad 20$$
$$= 22 + 2 = 24$$

We do not reduce the Master Numbers, 11, 22 and 33 (see p. 142).

So Steven John = 24/6.

The birth number is 32/5. We have chosen a name one higher, i.e. 6, to force development. The qualities of the birth number, in this case 32/5, are always strong, but Steven John adds 24/6 for extra strength and 1, 2, 5, 4, 5, 5, 1, 6, 8, 5 as support numbers. As we can see, there are plenty of 5s to strengthen the birth number, plus other numbers lacking in the date of birth.

Birth numbers: 9–1–1957 = 32/5. There are no 4s, 6s or 8s.

Steven John = 24/6, which gives us the missing 4s, 6s and
125455 1685   8s as support numbers, and we now have –

major numbers: 3–2–5 (d.o.b.) and 2–4–6 (name), missing 1, 7, 8, 9;

support numbers: 9–1–1957 and 1254551685 (these add the missing numbers).

NUMBER ONE QUALITIES

If your birth number reduces to a number One, it instils leadership, independence, originality and all things associated with the strong-minded and strong-willed pioneers of years gone by.

Like it or not, Ones prefer to give rather than receive orders, to lead rather than be led. This does not mean that all Ones are leaders in their jobs, careers or home life, or that they do not suffer the fears, apprehensions or worries of other numbers, only that if the circumstances allow and there is no one else around, they will out of necessity take command and create the peace and tranquility we all demand and require.

As the number says, Ones like to come first, so they tend to be that little bit more competitive or perhaps a little more willing to take that risk that others step back from.

Negative Ones want to give the orders without first earning the respect of their followers. They can become dictatorial and negative in their response to advice given, feeling that they are always right.

Ones are in tune with other Ones, Fours and Eights.

Any name of this vibration will strengthen the birth number and your child's personality. Or choose one of the three directional numbers (pp. 7–8).

TYPES OF ONES

10/1   A straightforward, to-the-point type, who speaks his or her mind and deals with problems on the spot. Prone to being honest but blunt.

19/1   A little more adventurous; desire for excitement can cause this number to take risks. Prone to being a practical joker. Can be hell if angered.

28/1   This is a softer type of One at home but a go-getter in the world of business and commerce. For a One, this person may appear slow but, be warned, it is a fact that he or she moves when sure of the kill.

37/1   This One is out for as much variety, fun and excitement as can be found. A sharp mind and intuition combined usually sees this number climb to the top. They somehow seem to achieve with less effort.

46/1   This is more of the domestic type of One who will direct more energy into home security and building rather than enterprise. Though a hard worker, there is no place like home for a 46/1.

55/1   This is a much rarer One in names and has the ability to communicate the subconscious to the conscious. It is neither masculine nor feminine and is not passionate or aggressive; it partakes of both, yet is neither.

NUMBER ONE NAMES – GIRLS

Name	Number	Total	Origins and Meanings
Adalia First vowel A – to lead	141391	19/1	Saxon tribal name, origins unknown.
Agnes First vowel A – to lead	17551	19/1	Greek. Pure, chaste, lamblike.
Aileen First vowel A – to lead	193555	28/1	Greek. A derivative of Helen.
Aleria First vowel A – to lead	135991	28/1	Latin. Eagle-like.
Aloha First vowel A – to lead	13681	19/1	Hawaiian greeting. A romantic name from the Hawaiian islands.
Anatola First vowel A – to lead	1512631	19/1	Greek. Woman of the East.
Armida First vowel A – to lead	194941	28/1	Latin. Small warrior.
Bertrade First vowel E – to communicate	25929145	37/1	Anglo-Saxon. Shining advisor.
Bronwen First vowel O – to study	2965555	37/1	Welsh/Celtic. White-bosomed.
Caledonia First vowel A – to lead	313546591	37/1	Latin. Scottish lassie.
Calypso First vowel A – to lead	3137716	28/1	Greek. Concealer, a legendary sea nymph.
Cameo First vowel A – to lead	31456	19/1	Italian. Sculptured jewel.
Ceara First vowel E – to communicate	35191	19/1	Irish. Spear.
Cilla First vowel I – intuition	39331	19/1	Latin. From Priscilla.
Cindy First vowel I – intuition	39547	28/1	Greek. Derived from Cynthia.
Clarissa First vowel A – to lead	33199111	28/1	French. Little shining one.

Clementine   3354552955   46/1
First vowel E – to communicate

Latin. Merciful and kind.

Cleopatra   335671291   37/1
First vowel E – to communicate

Greek. Her father's glory.

Concordia   365369491   46/1
First vowel O – to study

Latin. Harmony and peace.

Consolata   365163121   28/1
First vowel O – to study

Latin. One who consoles.

Cora   3691   19/1
First vowel O – to study

Greek. The maiden.

Daniela   4159531   28/1
First vowel A – to lead

Hebrew. 'God is my judge'. Feminine of Daniel.

Delphine   45378955   46/1
First vowel E – to communicate

Greek. Calmness and serenity.

Donata   465121   19/1
First vowel O – to study

Latin. The gift.

Eda   541   10/1
First vowel E – to communicate

Anglo-Saxon. Poetry.

Edith   54928   28/1
First vowel E – to communicate

Teutonic. Rich gift.

Elaine   531955   28/1
First vowel E – to communicate

Greek. Light.

Eldora   534691   28/1
First vowel E – to communicate

Spanish. Gilded one.

Electra   5353291   28/1
First vowel E – to communicate

Greek. Brilliant one.

Elfrida   5369941   37/1
First vowel E – to communicate

Teutonic. Elf strength.

Elinor   539569   37/1
First vowel E – to communicate

French. A form of Helen.

Elsa   5311   10/1
First vowel E – to communicate

Anglo-Saxon, or German form of Elizabeth.

Emily   54937   28/1
First vowel E – to communicate

Teutonic. Industrious.

Emogene   5467555   37/1
First vowel E – to communicate

Latin. Image of her mother.

Name	Number	Total	Origins and Meanings
Erin First vowel E – to communicate	5995	28/1	Gaelic. From Ireland.
Erma First vowel E – to communicate	5941	19/1	Teutonic. Army maid.
Ernestine First vowel E – to communicate	595512955	46/1	Anglo-Saxon. Purposeful one.
Eva First vowel E – to communicate	541	10/1	Hebrew. Life giver.
Fabia First vowel A – to lead	61291	19/1	Latin. Bean grower.
Faye First vowel E – to communicate	6175	19/1	French, a fairy. Or, Irish, a raven.
Felda First vowel E – to communicate	65341	19/1	Teutonic. From the field.
Fenella First vowel E – to communicate	6555331	28/1	Gaelic. White shouldered.
Feodora First vowel E – to communicate	6564691	37/1	Greek. Gift of gold.
Freya First vowel E – to communicate	69571	28/1	Norse. Noble goddess.
Gillian First vowel I – intuition	7933915	37/1	Latin. Young nestling.
Hannah First vowel A – to lead	815518	28/1	Hebrew. Full of grace.
Heloise First vowel E – to communicate	8536915	37/1	Teutonic (Louise). Battle maiden.
Henrietta First vowel E – to communicate	855995221	46/1	Teutonic. Ruler of home and estate.
Hilary First vowel I – intuition	893197	37/1	Latin. Cheerful one.
Iola First vowel I – intuition	9631	19/1	Greek. Colour of dawn cloud.
Iris First vowel I – intuition	9991	28/1	Greek. The rainbow.
Isleen First vowel I – intuition	913555	28/1	Gaelic (Aisleen). The vision.

Isolde	916345	28/1	Celtic. The fair
First vowel I – intuition			one.
Jayne	11755	19/1	Hebrew (Jane). God's
First vowel A – to lead			gift of grace.
Jerusha	1593181	28/1	Hebrew. The
First vowel E – to communicate			married one.
Jewel	15553	19/1	Latin. Most
First vowel E – to communicate			precious one.
Joanna	161551	19/1	Hebrew. God's gift
First vowel O – to study			of grace.
Joceline	16353955	37/1	Latin. Fair and just.
First vowel O – to study			Fem. of Justin.
Joselyn	1615375	28/1	Latin. Fair and just.
First vowel O – to study			Fem. of Justin.
Katherine	212859955	46/1	Greek. Pure
First vowel A – to lead			maiden.
Kay	217	10/1	Greek. 'Pure maiden'.
First vowel A – to lead			(From Catherine.)
Kimberley	294259357	46/1	English. From the
First vowel I – intuition			royal meadow.
Kirstie	2991295	37/1	Norse. The
First vowel I – intuition			annointed one.
Kirstin	2991295	37/1	Norse. The
First vowel I – intuition			annointed one.
Lalita	313921	19/1	Sanskrit. Without
First vowel A – to lead			guile.
Lana	3151	10/1	Celtic. Bright fair
First vowel A – to lead			one.
Leane	35155	19/1	French. 'The vine'.
First vowel E – to communicate			
Leatrice	35129935	37/1	Combination of
First vowel E – to communicate			Leah and Beatrice.
Liana	39151	19/1	French. The vine.
First vowel I – intuition			
Lois	3691	19/1	Teutonic. Famous
First vowel O – to study			battle maid.
Lora	3691	19/1	Latin (Laura). The
First vowel O – to study			laurel wreath.

Name	Number	Total	Origins and Meanings
Lucinda First vowel U – to protect	3339541	28/1	Latin. Light.
Madelaine First vowel A – to lead	414531955	37/1	Greek. Tower of strength.
Mae First vowel A – to lead	415	10/1	Latin (May). Born in May.
Maeve First vowel A – to lead	41545	19/1	Irish. The Warrior Queen of Connaught.
Maida First vowel A – to lead	41941	19/1	Anglo-Saxon. The maiden.
Maire First vowel A – to lead	41995	28/1	Irish form of Mary, 'bitterness'.
Marie First vowel A – to lead	41995	28/1	Hebrew. Bitterness.
Martita First vowel A – to lead	4192921	28/1	Arabic. Derived from Martha, 'the mistress'.
Mavis First vowel A – to lead	41491	19/1	French. Song thrush.
Maximilia First vowel A – to lead	416949391	46/1	Latin. The greatest.
Mertice First vowel E – to communicate	4592935	37/1	Anglo-Saxon. Famous and pleasant.
Meryl First vowel E – to communicate	45973	28/1	Latin (Merle). The blackbird.
Minerva First vowel I – intuition	4955941	37/1	Latin. Wise, purposeful one.
Monica First vowel O – to study	465931	28/1	Latin. Advice giver.
Musidora First vowel U – to protect	43194691	37/1	Greek. Gift of the Muses.
Natasha First vowel A – to lead	5121181	19/1	Latin. Born at Christmas time.
Neysa First vowel E – to communicate	55711	19/1	Greek (Agnes). Pure and chaste.
Noel First vowel O – to study	5653	19/1	Latin. Born at Christmas time.

Odelia	645391	28/1	Teutonic. Prosperous
First vowel O – to study			one.
Ordelia	6945391	37/1	Teutonic. Elf's spear.
First vowel O – to study			
Patience	71295535	37/1	Latin. Patient one.
First vowel A – to lead			
Perdita	7594921	37/1	Latin. The lost one.
First vowel E – to communicate			
Petronella	7529655331	46/1	Greek. Steadfast as a
First vowel E – to communicate			rock. Fem. of Peter.
Philberta	789325921	46/1	Teutonic. Very brilliant.
First vowel I – intuition			
Philomela	789364531	46/1	Greek. Lover of song.
First vowel I – intuition			
Phoenix	7865596	46/1	Greek. The eagle risen
First vowel O – to study			from ashes.
Piper	79759	37/1	English. Player of
First vowel I – intituion			pipes.
Placida	7313941	28/1	Latin. Peaceful one.
First vowel A – to lead			
Quinta	839521	28/1	Latin. The fifth child.
First vowel U – to protect			
Rebecca	9525331	28/1	Hebrew. Captivator.
First vowel E – to communicate			
Reva	9541	19/1	Latin. Strength
First vowel E – to communicate			regained.
Rhoda	98641	28/1	Greek. Garland of
First vowel O – to study			roses.
Roderica	96459931	46/1	Teutonic. Famous
First vowel O – to study			ruler.
Rosanna	9611551	28/1	English. Graceful rose.
First vowel O – to study			
Rosemund	96154354	37/1	French. Rose of the
First vowel O – to study			world.
Roxana	966151	28/1	Persian. Brilliant dawn.
First vowel O – to study			
Roxanne	9661555	37/1	Persian. Brilliant dawn.
First vowel O – to study			

Name	Number	Total	Origins and Meanings
Sabina First vowel A – to lead	112951	19/1	Latin. Woman of Sabine.
Sabrina First vowel A – to lead	1129951	28/1	Latin. A princess.
Salvia First vowel A – to lead	113491	19/1	Latin. Sage herb.
Seraphina First vowel E – to communicate	159178951	46/1	Hebrew. The ardent believer.
Sharleen First vowel A – to lead	18193555	37/1	Teutonic (Caroline). Woman born to command.
Sherrie First vowel E – to communicate	1859995	46/1	French. Beloved one.
Stacey First vowel A – to lead	121357	19/1	Derived from Anastasia or Eustacia.
Suzanne First vowel U – to protect	1381555	28/1	Hebrew. Graceful lily.
Tertia First vowel E – to communicate	259291	28/1	Latin. The third child.
Tessa First vowel E – to communicate	25111	10/1	Greek. The fourth child.
Thirza First vowel I – intuition	289981	37/1	Hebrew. Pleasantness.
Thomasina First vowel O – to study	286411951	37/1	Hebrew. The twin.
Timothea First vowel I – intuition	29462851	37/1	Greek. Honouring God.
Vera First vowel E – to communicate	4591	19/1	Latin. Truth, honesty.
Zandra First vowel A – to lead	815491	28/1	Greek. Helper of mankind.
Zara First vowel A – to lead	8191	19/1	Hebrew. Brightness of dawn.
Zena First vowel E – to communicate	8551	19/1	Greek. Hospitable one.
Zoe First vowel O – to study	865	19/1	Greek. Life.

NUMBER ONE NAMES – BOYS

Name	Number	Total	Origins and Meanings
Adam First vowel A – to lead	1414	10/1	Hebrew. Of the red earth.
Adin First vowel A – to lead	1495	19/1	Hebrew. Sensual.
Ahern First vowel A – to lead	18595	28/1	Gaelic. Horse owner.
Ahren First vowel A – to lead	18955	28/1	Teutonic. The eagle.
Alan First vowel A – to lead	1315	10/1	Gaelic. Cheerful harmony.
Aldrich First vowel A – to lead	1349938	37/1	Anglo-Saxon. Old, wise ruler.
Alfred First vowel A – to lead	136954	28/1	Anglo-Saxon. The wise counsel.
Allyn First vowel A – to lead	13375	19/1	Gaelic. Cheerful harmony.
Ambrose First vowel A – to lead	1429615	28/1	Latin. Belonging to immortals.
Aneurin First vowel A – to lead	1553995	37/1	Celtic. Truly gold.
Anselm First vowel A – to lead	151534	19/1	Teutonic. Divine helmet.
Anton First vowel A – to lead	15265	19/1	Latin. Of inestimable world.
Arnold First vowel A – to lead	195634	28/1	Teutonic. Strong as an eagle.
Arvin First vowel A – to lead	19495	28/1	Teutonic. Friend of the people.
Ashby First vowel A – to lead	11827	19/1	Anglo-Saxon. Ash Tree Farm.
Atwell First vowel A – to lead	125533	19/1	Anglo-Saxon. From the spring.
Barret First vowel A – to lead	219952	28/1	Anglo-Saxon. Glorious raven.

Name	Number	Total	Origins and Meanings
Barry First vowel A – to lead	21997	28/1	Gaelic. Spearlike.
Bartram First vowel A – to lead	2192914	28/1	Anglo-Saxon. Bright raven.
Beaumont First vowel E – to communicate	25134652	28/1	French. Beautiful mountain.
Beecher First vowel E – to communicate	2553859	37/1	Anglo-Saxon. One who lives by oak trees.
Bertrand First vowel E – to communicate	25929154	37/1	Anglo-Saxon. Bright raven.
Blakeley First vowel A – to lead	23125357	28/1	Anglo-Saxon. From the black meadow.
Blaze First vowel A – to lead	23185	19/1	Latin. Stammerer, or firebrand.
Boniface First vowel O – to study	26596135	37/1	Latin. One who does good.
Boyd First vowel O – to study	2674	19/1	Gaelic. Light-haired.
Brant First vowel A – to lead	29152	19/1	Anglo-Saxon. Fiery one.
Brice First vowel I – intuition	29935	28/1	Celtic. Ambitious and alert.
Buck First vowel U – to protect	2332	10/1	Anglo-Saxon. The buck deer.
Burgess First vowel U – to protect	2397511	28/1	Anglo-Saxon. Lives in a fort.
Burnett First vowel U – to protect	2395522	28/1	Anglo-Saxon. One with brown complexion.
Byrne First vowel E – to communicate	27955	28/1	Anglo-Saxon. From the brook.
Cadell First vowel A – to lead	314533	19/1	Celtic. Battle spirit.
Caley First vowel A – to lead	31357	19/1	Gaelic. Thin, slender.
Campbell First vowel A – to lead	31472533	28/1	Celtic. Crooked mouth.

Canute 315325 19/1 Norse. The knot.
First vowel A – to lead

Carvell 3194533 28/1 French. Estate in the
First vowel A – to lead marshes.

Chancellor 3815353369 46/1 Anglo-Saxon. King's
First vowel A – to lead counsellor.

Charlton 38193265 37/1 Anglo-Saxon. Charles's
First vowel A – to lead farm.

Chaunce 3813535 28/1 Anglo-Saxon. Good
First vowel A – to lead fortune.

Chuck 38332 19/1 Teutonic (Charles).
First vowel U – to protect Strong man.

Cleary 335197 28/1 Gaelic. The scholar.
First vowel E – to communicate

Clifford 33966694 46/1 Anglo-Saxon. From the
First vowel I – intuition ford by the cliff.

Colter 363259 28/1 Anglo-Saxon. The colt
First vowel O – to study herder.

Colum 36334 19/1 Latin. Dove.
First vowel O – to study

Conn 3655 19/1 Celtic. High.
First vowel O – to study

Conrad 365914 28/1 Teutonic. Brave
First vowel O – to study counsellor.

Corwin 369595 37/1 French. Friend of the
First vowel O – to study heart.

Danby 41527 19/1 Norse. From the Danish
First vowel A – to lead settlement.

Darrin 419995 37/1 Gaelic. Little great one.
First vowel A – to lead

Davis 41491 19/1 Anglo-Saxon. David's
First vowel A – to lead son.

Dempster 45471259 37/1 Anglo-Saxon. The
First vowel E – to communicate judge.

Derward 4595194 37/1 Anglo-Saxon. Guardian
First vowel E – to communicate of the deer.

Derwin 459595 37/1 Anglo-Saxon. Dearest
First vowel E – to communicate friend.

Name	Number	Total	Origins and Meanings
Dolan	46315	19/1	Gaelic. Black-haired.
First vowel O – to study			
Duff	4366	19/1	Gaelic. Dark
First vowel U – to protect			complexion.
Eaton	51265	19/1	Anglo-Saxon. From an
First vowel E – to communicate			estate by the river.
Eden	5455	19/1	Hebrew. Place of
First vowel E – to communicate			delight.
Edmond	544654	28/1	Anglo-Saxon. Rich
First vowel E – to communicate			guardian.
Edward	545194	28/1	Anglo-Saxon.
First vowel E – to communicate			Prosperous guardian.
Edwin	54595	28/1	Anglo-Saxon.
First vowel E – to communicate			Prosperous friend.
Elias	53911	19/1	Hebrew. 'The Lord is
First vowel E – to communicate			God'.
Elliot	533962	28/1	Hebrew. 'The Lord is
First vowel E – to communicate			God'.
Elvy	5347	19/1	Anglo-Saxon. Elfin
First vowel E – to communicate			warrior.
Emerick	5459932	37/1	Teutonic. Industrious
First vowel E – to communicate			ruler.
Erick	59932	28/1	Norse. All powerful
First vowel E – to communicate			ruler.
Everard	5459194	37/1	Anglo-Saxon. The
First vowel E – to communicate			strong bear.
Ezekiel	5852953	37/1	Hebrew. Strength of
First vowel E – to communicate			God.
Fitch	69238	28/1	Anglo-Saxon. The
First vowel I – intuition			marten.
Flinn	63955	28/1	Gaelic. Son of the
First vowel I – intuition			red-haired one.
Fremont	6954652	37/1	Teutonic. Free and
First vowel E – to communicate			noble protector.
Gawain	715195	28/1	Celtic. The battle hawk.
First vowel A – to lead			

Gaylord First vowel A – to lead	7173694	37/1	French. The happy nobleman.
Gilbert First vowel I – intuition	7932592	37/1	Anglo-Saxon. Bright pledge.
Gordon First vowel O – to study	769465	37/1	Anglo-Saxon. From the cornered hill.
Grady First vowel A – to lead	79147	28/1	Gaelic. Illustrious and noble.
Granville First vowel A – to lead	791549335	46/1	French. Dweller in a big town.
Grey First vowel E – to communicate	7957	28/1	Anglo-Saxon. The grey one.
Griff First vowel I – intuition	79966	37/1	Celtic. Fierce, red-haired warrior.
Hadley First vowel A – to lead	814357	28/1	Anglo-Saxon. From the heath meadow.
Harman First vowel A – to lead	819415	28/1	Teutonic. Army warrior.
Harris First vowel A – to lead	819991	37/1	Anglo-Saxon. Harold's son.
Hereward First vowel E – to communicate	85955194	46/1	Anglo-Saxon. Army guard.
Hezekiah First vowel E – to communicate	85852918	46/1	Hebrew. God is strength.
Hilary First vowel I – intuition	893197	37/1	Latin. Cheerful and merry.
Holt First vowel O – to study	8632	19/1	Anglo-Saxon. From the forest.
Humphry First vowel U – to protect	8347897	46/1	Teutonic. Protector of the peace.
Hywel First vowel E – to communicate	87553	28/1	Celtic. Little alert one.
Ignatius First vowel I – intuition	97512931	37/1	Latin. The ardent one.
Ira First vowel I – intuition	991	19/1	Hebrew. The watcher.
Irwin First vowel I – intuition	99595	37/1	Anglo-Saxon. Sea friend.

Name	Number	Total	Origins and Meanings
Israel First vowel I – intuition	919153	28/1	Hebrew. The Lord's soldier.
Ivan First vowel I – intuition	9415	19/1	Hebrew (John). God's gracious gift.
Ives First vowel I – intuition	9451	19/1	Anglo-Saxon. Son of the archer.
Ivo First vowel I – intuition	946	19/1	Latin form of Ives.
Ivor First vowel I – intuition	9469	28/1	Norse. Battle archer.
Jedediah First vowel E – to communicate	15454918	37/1	Hebrew. Beloved of the Lord.
Jerrold First vowel E – to communicate	1599634	37/1	Teutonic. Mighty spear warrior.
Joseph First vowel O – to study	161578	28/1	Hebrew. He shall add.
Kay First vowel A – to lead	217	10/1	Celtic. Rejoiced in.
Kelvin First vowel E – to communicate	253495	28/1	Gaelic. From the narrow stream.
Keye First vowel E – to communicate	2575	19/1	Gaelic. Son of the fiery one.
Knox First vowel O – to study	2566	19/1	Anglo-Saxon. From the hills.
Kyne First vowel E – to communicate	2755	19/1	Anglo-Saxon. The royal one.
Lancelot First vowel A – to lead	31535362	28/1	French. Spear attendant.
Latham First vowel A – to lead	312814	19/1	Anglo-Saxon. From the barns.
Leon First vowel E – to communicate	3565	19/1	French. Lionlike.
Link First vowel I – intuition	3952	19/1	Anglo-Saxon. From the bank.
Locke First vowel O – to study	36325	19/1	Anglo-Saxon. Dweller in the stronghold.

Loren 36955 28/1 Latin. Crowned with
First vowel O – to study laurels.

Lyndsay 3754117 28/1 Anglo-Saxon. Pool
First vowel A – to lead island.

Marden 419455 28/1 Anglo-Saxon. From the
First vowel A – to lead pool in the valley.

Marlon 419365 28/1 Anglo-Saxon (Merlin).
First vowel A – to lead The falcon.

Marlow 419365 28/1 Anglo-Saxon. From the
First vowel A – to lead lake on the hill.

Martyn 419275 28/1 Latin. Warlike.
First vowel A – to lead

Melvil 453493 28/1 French. From the estate
First vowel E – to communicate of the industrious.

Melvyn 453475 28/1 Anglo-Saxon. Famous
First vowel E – to communicate friend.

Mitchell 49238533 37/1 Hebrew. Like unto the
First vowel I – intuition Lord.

Montgomery 4652764597 55/1 French. The mountain
First vowel O – to study hunter.

Murdoch 4394638 37/1 Celtic. Prosperous from
First vowel U – to protect the sea.

Neale 55135 19/1 Gaelic. The champion.
First vowel E – to communicate

Nestor 551269 28/1 Greek. Ancient wisdom.
First vowel E – to communicate

Nevin 55495 28/1 Gaelic. Worshipper of
First vowel E – to communicate saints.

Nicolas 5936311 28/1 Greek. The leader of
First vowel I – intuition the people.

Noel 5653 19/1 French. Born at
First vowel O – to study Christmas.

Oxford 666694 37/1 Anglo-Saxon. From the
First vowel O – to study ford where oxen cross.

Park 7192 19/1 Anglo-Saxon. From the
First vowel A – to lead park.

Padgett 7147522 28/1 French. Page, young
First vowel A – to lead attendant.

Name	Number	Total	Origins and Meanings
Perceval First vowel E – to communicate	75935413	37/1	French. Valley piercer.
Pernell First vowel E – to communicate	7595533	37/1	Latin. The rock. A form of Peter.
Perry First vowel E – to communicate	75997	37/1	Anglo-Saxon. From the pear tree. Also dim. of Peregrine.
Peter First vowel E – to communicate	75259	28/1	Greek. The stone/rock.
Peverall First vowel E – to communicate	75459133	37/1	French. The piper.
Phillip First vowel I – intuition	7893397	46/1	Greek. Lover of horses.
Quentin First vowel U – to protect	8355295	37/1	Latin. The fifth born.
Quillon First vowel U – to protect	8393365	37/1	Latin. The sword.
Ralf First vowel A – to lead	9136	19/1	Anglo-Saxon. Counsel wolf.
Ralph First vowel A – to lead	91378	28/1	Anglo-Saxon. Counsel wolf.
Rand First vowel A – to lead	9154	19/1	Old English. Shield wolf.
Raynor First vowel A – to lead	917569	37/1	Scandinavian. Mighty army.
Read First vowel E – to communicate	9514	19/1	Anglo-Saxon. The red-headed one.
Redman First vowel E – to communicate	954415	28/1	Anglo-Saxon. Protector and advisor.
Redmond First vowel E – to communicate	9544654	37/1	Anglo-Saxon. Protector and advisor.
Redvers First vowel E – to communicate	9544591	37/1	Anglo-Saxon. From the red ford.
Reede First vowel E – to communicate	95545	28/1	Anglo-Saxon. The red-headed one.
Reeve First vowel E – to communicate	95545	28/1	Anglo-Saxon. The steward.

Ridley 994357 37/1 Anglo-Saxon. From the
First vowel I – intuition red meadow.

Robb 9622 19/1 Teutonic. Bright fame.
First vowel O – to study

Rogan 96715 28/1 Gaelic. Red-haired one.
First vowel O – to study

Roland 963154 28/1 Teutonic. From famed
First vowel O – to study land.

Ronald 965134 28/1 Teutonic. Mighty and
First vowel O – to study powerful ruler.

Rushford 93186694 46/1 Anglo-Saxon. From the
First vowel U – to protect rush ford.

Saxon 11665 19/1 Anglo-Saxon. People of
First vowel A – to lead the swords.

Sherlock 18593632 37/1 Anglo-Saxon.
First vowel E – to communicate White-haired man.

Siegfried 195769954 55/1 Teutonic. Bright fame.
First vowel I – intuition

Skip 1297 19/1 Anglo-Saxon. From the
First vowel I – intuition sheep farm.

Stacey 121357 19/1 Latin. Prosperous and
First vowel A – to lead stable.

Sutton 132265 19/1 Anglo-Saxon. From the
First vowel U – to protect south of town.

Sylvester 173451259 37/1 Latin (Silas). From the
First vowel E – to communicate forest.

Tate 2125 10/1 Anglo-Saxon. Cheerful.
First vowel A – to lead

Taylor 217369 28/1 Anglo-Saxon. The
First vowel A – to lead tailor.

Thaddeus 28144531 28/1 Hebrew, praise to God.
First vowel A – to lead Greek, courageous.

Thorpe 286975 37/1 Anglo-Saxon. From the
First vowel O – to study small village.

Tristram 29912914 37/1 Celtic. The sorrowful
First vowel I – intuition one.

True 2935 19/1 Latin. Honest, loyal.
First vowel U – to protect

Name	Number	Total	Origins and Meanings
Tynam	27514	19/1	Gaelic. Dark grey.
First vowel A – to lead			
Vaughn	413785	28/1	Celtic. The small one.
First vowel A – to lead			
Vergil	459793	37/1	Latin. Strong and
First vowel E – to communicate			flourishing.
Waldo	51346	19/1	Teutonic. Ruler.
First vowel A – to lead			
Ward	5194	19/1	Anglo-Saxon.
First vowel A – to lead			Watchman.
Weldon	553465	28/1	Anglo-Saxon. From the
First vowel E – to communicate			well on the hill.
Winfield	59569534	46/1	Anglo-Saxon. From a
First vowel I – intuition			friend's field.
Yules	73351	19/1	Anglo-Saxon. Born at
First vowel U – to protect			Christmas.
Zachary	8138197	37/1	Hebrew. 'The Lord has
First vowel A – to lead			remembered'.
Zane	8155	19/1	Hebrew (John). God's
First vowel A – to lead			gracious gift.

NUMBER TWO QUALITIES

If you were born with the number two as a birth number you are more in need of partnerships, company and compassion. Two as a vibration stands for the duality of give and take. It strengthens the desire for emotional expression and the need to help others to understand themselves, and, in so doing, gives the ruling Two a purpose in his or her life.

Twos feel the needs of their fellow man, their intuition and insight are strong and there is a great deal of compassion just waiting to find an outlet.

Keywords for Twos are Duality, Compassion, Caring, Loyalty, Sharing, Unselfishness and Femininity.

The negative Two can be mistrustful of other people's reasoning and ideology. This can, at its worst, force him into seclusion. Though desiring a mate to share his feelings, he lacks the confidence to trust anyone enough for that final long-term commitment he desires.

Twos get on best with other Twos, Fives and Sevens.

Any name of this vibration will strengthen the birth number and your child's personality. Or choose one of the three directional vibrations (pp. 7–8).

TYPES OF TWOS

11/2   See Master Numbers, pp. 142–3.

20/2   This type of Two seeks straightforward, direct, no-problem partnerships. It feels a need to share, and finds its opposite to share with, be it love, work or fun.

29/2   This type of Two is a little more aggressive about how or what takes place in its chosen field or partnerships and can be at times outspoken if it feels neglected or misused.

38/2   Blends philosophy and good business sense while still remaining able to enjoy other facets of our lifestyles that we call fun. Such Twos can show a tendency towards flirtatious or mischievous acts, though the number is very loyal.

47/2   Needs to build upon and improve what he or she already has. The imagination of the 7 can become the reality of the 4 through a stable partnership.

65/2   Is quite rare in name numbers and is indicative of a need to share with the world as a whole. Charitable and hospitable acts could come from a 65/2.

74/2   We know of no name examples as singular names.

NUMBER TWO NAMES – GIRLS

Name	Number	Total	Origins and Meanings
Adina First vowel A – to lead	14951	20/2	Hebrew. Voluptuous one, of ripe mature charm.
Agatha First vowel A – to lead	171281	20/2	Greek. One of strong good virtue.
Aisleen First vowel A – to lead	1913555	29/2	Gaelic. The vision.
Alfreda First vowel A – to lead	1369541	29/2	Teutonic. Wise counsellor.
Alpha First vowel A – to lead	13781	20/2	Greek. First one.
Althea First vowel A – to lead	132851	20/2	Greek. The healer.
Amaryllis First vowel A – to lead	141973391	38/2	Greek. From the flower of this name.
Ann First vowel A – to lead	155	11/2	Hebrew. Full of grace.
Antonia First vowel A – to lead	1526591	29/2	Latin. Beyond price, excellent.
April First vowel A – to lead	17993	29/2	Latin. The month.
Arabelle First vowel A – to lead	19125335	29/2	Latin. Beautiful altar.
Audrey First vowel A – to lead	134957	29/2	Anglo-Saxon. Strong and noble.
Aurora First vowel A – to lead	139691	29/2	Latin. Day-break.
Belinda First vowel E – to communicate	2539541	29/2	Latin. Wise and immortal beauty.
Bernice First vowel E – to communicate	2595935	38/2	Greek. Herald of victory.
Bridget First vowel I – intuition	2994752	38/2	Irish/Celtic. Strong and mighty.

Name	Number	Total	Origins and Meanings
Briony 299657 First vowel I – intuition		38/2	Old English. The twisting vine.
Brunetta 29355221 First vowel U – to protect		29/2	French. Dark-haired maiden.
Calista 3139121 First vowel A – to lead		20/2	Greek. Most beautiful woman.
Candy 31547 First vowel A – to lead		20/2	Latin. Pure; brilliant white.
Cassie 311195 First vowel A – to lead		20/2	Latin. Prophetess.
Catherine 312859955 First vowel A – to lead		47/2	Greek. Pure maiden.
Clytie 337295 First vowel I – intuition		29/2	Greek. Splendid daughter.
Conradine 365914955 First vowel O – to study		47/2	Teutonic. Bold and wise.
Corinna 3699551 First vowel O – to study		38/2	Greek. The maiden.
Damaris 4141991 First vowel A – to lead		29/2	Greek. A calf.
Denise 455915 First vowel E – to communicate		29/2	French. Wine goddess.
Desiree 4519955 First vowel E – to communicate		38/2	French. Desired one.
Diana 49151 First vowel I – intuition		20/2	Latin. Moon goddess.
Dione 49655 First vowel I – intuition		29/2	Greek. Daughter of Heaven and Earth.
Domina 464951 First vowel O – to study		29/2	Latin. A noble lady.
Dora 4691 First vowel O – to study		20/2	Greek. Gift of God.
Dorinda 4699541 First vowel O – to study		38/2	Greek/Spanish. Beautiful golden gift.
Doris 46991 First vowel O – to study		29/2	Greek. From the sea.

Edmonda 5446541 29/2 Anglo-Saxon. Rich
First vowel E – to communicate protector.

Edwina 545951 29/2 Anglo-Saxon. Rich
First vowel E – to communicate friend.

Eloise 536915 29/2 Hebrew. Noble one.
First vowel E – to communicate

Erna 5951 20/2 Anglo-Saxon. Eagle.
First vowel E – to communicate

Estella 5125331 20/2 French. Bright star.
First vowel E – to communicate

Evelyn 545375 29/2 Hebrew. Life giver.
First vowel E – to communicate

Gail 7193 20/2 Hebrew (Abigail).
First vowel A – to lead Father rejoiced.

Garnet 719552 29/2 English. Deep
First vowel A – to lead red-haired beauty.

Gleda 73541 20/2 Anglo-Saxon. Old
First vowel E – to communicate English version of
Gladys.

Gypsy 77717 29/2 Anglo-Saxon. The
No vowel, I sound wanderer.

Heather 8512859 38/2 Anglo-Saxon. Flower of
First vowel E – to communicate the moors.

Hebe 8525 20/2 Greek. Goddess of
First vowel E – to communicate youth.

Isis 9191 20/2 Egyptian. Supreme
First vowel I – intuition goddess.

Isola 91631 20/2 Latin. Isolated one. A
First vowel I – intuition loner.

Ivy 947 20/2 English. The ivy plant.
First vowel I – intuition

Jacinth 1139528 29/2 Greek (Hyacinth). A
First vowel A – to lead flower.

Joletta 1635221 20/2 Latin (Julia). Youthful.
First vowel O – to study

Josceline 161353955 38/2 Latin. Fair and just.
First vowel O – to study Fem. of Justin.

Name	Number	Total	Origins and Meanings
Josephine	161578955	47/2	Hebrew. She shall add.
First vowel O – to study			
Katrina	2129951	29/2	Greek. Pure maiden.
First vowel A – to lead			
Leona	35651	20/2	Latin. Lioness.
First vowel E – to communicate			
Lettice	3522935	29/2	Latin. Joyous gladness.
First vowel E – to communicate			
Lilliane	39339155	38/2	Latin. A lily.
First vowel I – intuition			
Linnet	395552	29/2	French. Sweet bird.
First vowel I – intuition			
Lorena	369551	29/2	Latin (Laura). Laurel wreath.
First vowel O – to study			
Lorraine	36991955	47/2	Teutonic. Renowned in battle.
First vowel O – to study			
Lucille	3339335	29/2	Latin. Light.
First vowel U – to protect			
Lynda	37541	20/2	Spanish. Pretty one.
First vowel A – to lead			
Lynn	3755	20/2	Celtic. A waterfall.
No vowel, I sound			
Maisie	419195	29/2	Latin (Margaret). A pearl.
First vowel A – to lead			
Margaret	41971952	38/2	Latin. A pearl.
First vowel A – to lead			
Margot	419762	29/2	Latin. A pearl.
First vowel A – to lead			
Marian	419915	29/2	Hebrew. Graceful.
First vowel A – to lead			
Marilyn	4199375	38/2	Hebrew. Bitterness.
First vowel A – to lead			
Marina	419951	29/2	Latin. Lady of the sea.
First vowel A – to lead			
Melantha	45315281	29/2	Greek. Lady of the night.
First vowel E – to communicate			

Melody 453647 29/2 Greek. Like a song.
First vowel E – to communicate

Mildred 4934954 38/2 Anglo-Saxon. Gentle
First vowel I – intuition counsellor.

Modesty 4645127 29/2 Latin. Shy, modest.
First vowel O – to study

Moira 46991 29/2 Celtic (Morag). Great.
First vowel O – to study

Nadia 51491 20/2 French. Hope.
First vowel A – to lead

Nadine 514955 29/2 French. Hope.
First vowel A – to lead

Nina 5951 20/2 Spanish. The daughter.
First vowel I – intuition

Norah 56918 29/2 Latin. Derived from
First vowel O – to study Honora.

Phyllis 7873391 38/1 Greek. The green
First vowel I – intuition bough.

Pomona 764651 29/2 Latin. Fruitful and
First vowel O – to study fertile.

Rachel 913853 29/2 Hebrew. Innocent as a
First vowel A – to lead lamb.

Raine 91955 29/2 Latin. A queen (derived
First vowel A – to lead from Regina).

Raquel 918353 29/2 Hebrew. Innocent as a
First vowel A – to lead lamb.

Rhona 98651 29/2 Gaelic. A seal.
First vowel O – to study

Rolanda 9631541 29/2 Teutonic. From the
First vowel O – to study famed land.

Roma 9641 20/2 Latin. Woman of Rome.
First vowel O – to study

Ronalda 9651341 29/2 Teutonic. All powerful.
First vowel O – to study

Rosalind 96113954 38/2 Latin. Fair and beautiful
First vowel O – to study rose.

Sadie 11495 20/2 Hebrew (Sarah). One of
First vowel A – to lead royal blood.

Name	Number	Total	Origins and Meanings
Salina First vowel A – to lead	113951	20/2	Greek. From the salty place.
Salome First vowel A – to lead	113645	20/2	Hebrew. Peace.
Sarah First vowel A – to lead	11918	20/2	Hebrew. Princess, one of royal status.
Saxona First vowel A – to lead	116651	20/2	Teutonic. Sword bearer.
Selena First vowel E – to communicate	153551	20/2	Greek. The Moon.
Sonya First vowel O – to study	16571	20/2	Greek. Wisdom.
Titania First vowel I – intuition	2921591	29/2	Greek. Giantess, or Queen of the Fairies.
Tracie First vowel A – to lead	291395	29/2	Gaelic. Battler. Also derived from Teresa.
Ursula First vowel U – to protect	391331	20/2	Latin. The she bear.
Ventura First vowel E – to communicate	4552391	29/2	Spanish. Happiness, good luck.
Violet First vowel I – intuition	496352	29/2	Latin. Modest flower.
Warda First vowel A – to lead	51941	20/2	Teutonic. Guardian.
Winola First vowel I – intuition	595631	29/2	Teutonic. Gracious friend.
Zona First vowel O – to study	8651	20/2	Latin. A girdle, belt of Orion.

Note: Refer to the section on Master Numbers 11 for Girls (p. 144) for a further selection of Two names.

NUMBER TWO NAMES – BOYS

Name	Number	Total	Origins and Meanings
Adrian First vowel A – to lead	149915	29/2	Latin. Dark one, man of the sea.
Aidan First vowel A – to lead	19415	20/2	Gaelic. Little fairy one.
Albin First vowel A – to lead	13295	20/2	Latin (Alban). White complexion.
Andrew First vowel A – to lead	154955	29/2	Greek. Strong and manly.
Ardley First vowel A – to lead	194357	29/2	Anglo-Saxon. From the domestic meadow.
Atherton First vowel A – to lead	12859265	38/2	Anglo-Saxon. Dweller of the spring farm.
Aubin First vowel A – to lead	13295	20/2	French. The blond one.
Baldemar First vowel A – to lead	21345419	29/2	Teutonic. Bold and famous prince.
Baldwin First vowel A – to lead	2134595	29/2	Teutonic. Bold, noble protector.
Barney First vowel A – to lead	219557	29/2	Hebrew, son of consolation.
Bartley First vowel A – to lead	2192357	29/2	Anglo-Saxon. Bartholomew's meadow.
Beresford First vowel E – to communicate	259516694	47/2	Anglo-Saxon. From the barley wood.
Brett First vowel E – to communicate	29522	20/2	Celtic. Native of Brittany.
Burdon First vowel U – to protect	239465	29/2	Anglo-Saxon. One who lives by the castle on the hill.
Burley First vowel U – to protect	239357	29/2	Anglo-Saxon. Dweller in the castle by the meadow.

Name	Number	Total	Origins and Meanings
Byron First vowel O – to study	27965	29/2	French. From the cottage, or the bear.
Caesar First vowel A – to lead	315119	20/2	Latin. Emperor.
Caradock First vowel A – to lead	31914632	29/2	Celtic. Beloved.
Carlton First vowel A – to lead	3193265	29/2	Anglo-Saxon. Farmers' meeting place.
Cary First vowel A – to lead	3197	20/2	Celtic. One who lives by a castle.
Chapman First vowel A – to lead	3817415	29/2	Anglo-Saxon. The merchant.
Christian First vowel I – intuition	389912915	47/2	Latin. Believer in Christ.
Christmas First vowel I – intuition	389912411	38/2	Old English. Born at Christmas.
Cleve First vowel E – to communicate	33545	20/2	Anglo-Saxon. Cliff.
Collier First vowel O – to study	3633959	38/2	Anglo-Saxon. The charcoal maker.
Conan First vowel O – to study	36515	20/2	Celtic. High and mighty.
Corbett First vowel O – to study	3692522	29/2	French. The raven.
Cosmo First vowel O – to study	36146	20/2	Greek. The perfect order of the Universe.
Cowan First vowel O – to study	36515	20/2	Gaelic. Hollow in the hillside.
Craig First vowel A – to lead	39197	29/2	Celtic. From the stony hill.
Dacey First vowel A – to lead	41357	20/2	Gaelic. The southerner.
Daley First vowel A – to lead	41357	20/2	Gaelic. Counsellor.
Damon First vowel A – to lead	41465	20/2	Greek. The true friend.

Delwyn 453575 29/2
First vowel E – to communicate
Anglo-Saxon. Bright friend from the valley.

Dennis 455591 29/2
First vowel E – to communicate
Greek (Dionysus). Wine lover.

Derk 4592 20/2
First vowel E – to communicate
Teutonic. Ruler of the people.

Desmond 4514654 29/2
First vowel E – to communicate
Gaelic. Man of the world.

Dugan 43715 20/2
First vowel U – to protect
Gaelic. Dark skinned.

Dylan 47315 20/2
First vowel A – to lead
Welsh. Man from the sea.

Elson 53165 20/2
First vowel E – to communicate
Anglo-Saxon. Son of Elias.

Elwood 535664 29/2
First vowel E – to communicate
Anglo-Saxon. From the ancient forest.

Erling 593957 38/2
First vowel E – to communicate
Anglo-Saxon. Son of a nobleman.

Eustace 5312135 20/2
First vowel E – to communicate
Greek. Stable and tranquil.

Everley 5459357 38/2
First vowel E – to communicate
Anglo-Saxon. Field of the wild boar.

Ewen 5555 20/2
First vowel E – to communicate
Gaelic. Well born young warrior.

Fagan 61715 20/2
First vowel A – to lead
Gaelic. The fiery one.

Fairfax 6199616 38/2
First vowel A – to lead
Anglo-Saxon. Fair haired one.

Farold 619634 29/2
First vowel A – to lead
Anglo-Saxon. Mighty traveller.

Felix 65396 29/2
First vowel E – to communicate
Latin. Fortunate.

Fenton 655265 29/2
First vowel E – to communicate
Anglo-Saxon. Lives by marshland.

Flann 63155 20/2
First vowel A – to lead
Gaelic. One with red hair.

Forbes 669251 29/2
First vowel O – to study
Gaelic. Man of wealth, owner of land.

Name	Number	Total	Origins and Meanings
Frager First vowel A – to lead	691859	38/2	French. Strawberry, or curly-haired.
Franklyn First vowel A – to lead	69152375	38/2	Anglo-Saxon. Free-holder of property.
Fredrick First vowel E – to communicate	69549932	47/2	Teutonic. Peaceful ruler.
Frick First vowel I – intuition	69932	29/2	Anglo-Saxon. Bold man.
Fuller First vowel U – to protect	633359	29/2	Anglo-Saxon. Cloth thickener.
Galvin First vowel A – to lead	713495	29/2	Gaelic. Bright shining white.
Gannon First vowel A – to lead	715565	29/2	Gaelic. Little blond one.
Garey First vowel A – to lead	71957	29/2	Anglo-Saxon (Gary). Spearman.
Garnet First vowel A – to lead	719552	29/2	Latin. The red seed.
Geraint First vowel E – to communicate	7591952	38/2	Celtic. Old.
Gerald First vowel E – to communicate	759134	29/2	Teutonic. Mighty spear ruler.
Gifford First vowel I – intuition	7966694	47/2	Teutonic. The gift.
Glen First vowel E – to communicate	7355	20/2	Celtic. From the valley.
Griffith First vowel I – intuition	79966928	56/2	Celtic. Fierce red-haired warrior.
Gwynn No vowel, I sound	75755	29/2	Celtic. The blond one.
Hardy First vowel A – to lead	81947	29/2	Teutonic. Bold and daring.
Hart First vowel A – to lead	8192	20/2	Anglo-Saxon. The hart deer.
Hawley First vowel A – to lead	815357	29/2	Anglo-Saxon. From the hedged meadow.

Herbert 8592592 40/2
First vowel E – to communicate

Teutonic. Brilliant warrior.

Hubert 832592 29/2
First vowel U – to protect

Teutonic. Brilliant shining mind.

Hymen 87455 29/2
First vowel E – to communicate

Hebrew. Life.

Ingelbert 957532592 47/2
First vowel I – intuition

Teutonic. Brilliant angel.

Jared 11954 20/2
First vowel A – to lead

Hebrew. The descendant.

John 1685 20/2
First vowel O – to study

Hebrew. God's gracious gift.

Jonathan 16512815 29/2
First vowel O – to study

Hebrew. Gift of God.

Isidor 919469 38/2
First vowel I – intuition

Greek. The gift of Isis.

Joshua 161831 20/2
First vowel O – to study

Hebrew. God's salvation.

Julius 133931 20/2
First vowel U – to protect

Latin. Youthful.

Kelly 25337 20/2
First vowel E – to communicate

Gaelic. Warrior.

Kynan 27515 20/2
First vowel A – to lead

Celtic (Conan). High and mighty.

Lennon 355565 29/2
First vowel E – to communicate

Gaelic. Little cloak.

Lombard 3642194 29/2
First vowel O – to study

Latin. Long-bearded one.

Lothar 362819 29/2
First vowel O – to study

Teutonic. Famous warrior.

Lynn 3755 20/2
No vowel, I sound

Welsh. From the pool or waterfall.

Mario 41996 29/2
First vowel A – to lead

Latin. The martial one.

Marley 419357 29/2
First vowel A – to lead

Anglo-Saxon. From the meadow lake.

Milton 493265 29/2
First vowel I – intuition

Anglo-Saxon. From the mill town.

Name	Number	Total	Origins and Meanings
Morris 469991 First vowel O – to study		38/2	Latin. Moorish looking, dark skinned.
Myles 47351 First vowel E – to communicate		20/2	Latin. The soldier.
Nairn 51995 First vowel A – to lead		29/2	Celtic. Dweller by the alder tree.
Nemo 5546 First vowel E – to communicate		20/2	Greek. From the glen.
Nigel 59753 First vowel I – intuition		29/2	Latin. Black haired one.
Noah 5618 First vowel O – to study		20/2	Hebrew. Rest, comfort and peace.
Nolan 56315 First vowel O – to study		20/2	Latin. Famous.
Norbert 5692592 First vowel O – to study		38/2	Teutonic. Brilliant sea hero.
Omar 6419 First vowel O – to study		20/2	Arabic. The first son, religious follower.
Oram 6914 First vowel O – to study		20/2	Anglo-Saxon. Riverbank enclosure.
Orestes 6951251 First vowel O – to study		29/2	Greek. Mountain climber.
Oscar 61319 First vowel O – to study		20/2	Anglo-Saxon. Divine spearman, God's fighter.
Oswald 615134 First vowel O – to study		20/2	Anglo-Saxon. Divinely powerful.
Padraig 7149197 First vowel A – to lead		38/2	Latin. One of noble birth.
Palmer 713459 First vowel A – to lead		29/2	Latin. Palm-bearing pilgrim.
Phelan 785315 First vowel E – to communicate		29/2	Gaelic. Brave as a wolf.
Pierce 795935 First vowel I – intuition		38/2	Latin. The rock. A form of Peter.
Rainer 919559 First vowel A – to lead		38/2	Scandinavian. Mighty army.

Reuben	953255	29/2	Hebrew. 'Behold a son'.
First vowel E – to communicate			
Rex	956	20/2	Latin. King, all-powerful.
First vowel E – to communicate			
Rich	9938	29/2	Teutonic (Richard). Wealthy.
First vowel I – intuition			
Rock	9632	20/2	Anglo-Saxon. From the rock.
First vowel O – to study			
Roderick	96459932	47/2	Teutonic. Famous rich ruler.
First vowel O – to study			
Shane	18155	20/2	Hebrew (John). God's gracious gift.
First vowel A – to lead			
Shepherd	18578594	47/2	Anglo-Saxon. The sheep-tender.
First vowel E – to communicate			
Skeeter	1255259	29/2	Anglo-Saxon. The swift.
First vowel E – to communicate			
Sydney	174557	29/2	French. A follower of St. Denis.
First vowel E – to communicate			
Timothy	2946287	38/2	Greek. Honouring God.
First vowel I – intuition			
Tristan	2991215	29/2	Celtic. The noisy one.
First vowel I – intuition			
Urban	39215	20/2	Latin. From the city.
First vowel U – to protect			
Vaughan	4137815	29/2	Celtic. The small one.
First vowel A – to lead			
Wiley	59357	29/2	Teutonic (William). Determined protector.
First vowel I – intuition			
Will	5933	20/2	Teutonic (William). Determined protector.
First vowel I – intuition			
Wylie	57395	29/2	Anglo-Saxon. The enchanter.
First vowel I – intuition			
Zeke	8525	20/2	Hebrew (Ezekiel). Strength of God.
First vowel E – to communicate			

Note: Refer to the section on Master Numbers 11 for Boys (p. 145) for a further selection of Two names.

NUMBER THREE QUALITIES

If your birth number reduces to a Three it instils qualities of communication, expression, changeability and the ability to adapt to the surroundings you find yourself in. Self-expression and the urge to explore the unknown are qualities of a Three.

Three as a base number can at times have itchy feet. A Three throws himself whole-heartedly into projects but can find himself bored with what he is doing, and the longer he does one thing, the more he seeks to do something else.

Threes are communicators and there may be an artistic side to their characters also. Many threes become actors or salesmen as these professions can give them new roles or locations in their careers and supply the change and diversity that their inner selves crave for. Money and finance seem to come easy for a Three but so does the ability to spend what is earned as they enjoy life to the full and would rather live for today than for the fear of what may happen tomorrow.

Negative Threes fail to accept responsibility for their lifestyle and may run away from long-term commitments. Seekers of pleasure rarely have staying power.

Threes get on best with other Threes, Sixes or Nines.

Any name of this vibration will strengthen the birth number and your child's personality. Or choose one of the three directional numbers (pp. 7–8).

TYPES OF THREES

12/3   A blend of conscious and subconscious, able to understand and supply the needs of his fellow man. Good public speakers and able to express their true feelings.

21/3   As above, though when the 2 is first there is a tendency to an initial shyness or hesitation before action is taken. This type of Three needs to know you a little longer before he will commit himself.

30/3   The straight Three is as in Three Qualities (p. 48), straightforward and to the point. Live hard, play hard, work hard is the basis of life.

39/3   This type of Three is a little more physically active and may be seen on many sports fields or taking an active or energetic role in whatever takes his or her fancy. Not a sit down and watch type.

48/3   This is by far the quietest type of Three. He tends to plan more what he is going to do rather than to react to the circumstances like his fellow Threes. But beware when he is ready to move; there is little that can stop him.

57/3   Great communicative ability with this Three, coupled with a vivid imagination. This can be a great combination for work in design or artistic fields – the communication of the imagination to the reality.

66/3   Few names go this high by number. This type of Three can be very esoteric, caring and compassionate, wanting to bring joy, peace and happiness to those who understand his unusual philosophy.

NUMBER THREE NAMES – GIRLS

Name	Number	Total	Origins and Meanings
Adolpha First vowel A – to lead	1463781	30/3	Teutonic. Noble she wolf.
Albina First vowel A – to lead	132951	21/3	Latin. White lady.
Alice First vowel A – to lead	13935	21/3	Greek. Truth.
Amber First vowel A – to lead	14259	21/3	Arabic. A jewel.
Amethyst First vowel A – to lead	14528712	30/3	Greek. Semi-precious stone.
Amy First vowel A – to lead	147	12/3	French. Beloved friend.
Anna First vowel A – to lead	1551	12/3	Hebrew. Full of grace.
Annabelle First vowel A – to lead	155125335	30/3	Combination of Anna and Belle.
Argenta First vowel A – to lead	1975521	30/3	Latin. Silvery one.
Beda First vowel E – to communicate	2541	12/3	Anglo-Saxon. Warrior maiden.
Bee First vowel E – to communicate	255	12/3	Latin. Derived from Beatrice.
Candice First vowel A – to lead	3154935	30/3	Latin. Pure white.
Cecily First vowel E – to communicate	353937	30/3	Latin. The patron saint of music.
Celia First vowel E – to communicate	35391	21/3	Latin. Derived from Cecilia, the patron saint of music.
Charity First vowel A – to lead	3819927	39/3	Latin. Benevolent and loving.

Charleen	38193555	39/3	Teutonic (Caroline).
First vowel A – to lead			Little woman born to command.
Charlene	38193555	39/3	Teutonic. Little woman
First vowel A – to lead			born to command.
Charlotte	381936225	39/3	Teutonic. Little woman
First vowel A – to lead			born to command.
Cherie	385995	39/3	French. Dear beloved
First vowel E – to communicate			one.
Christiana	3899129151	48/3	Greek. Believer in
First vowel I – intuition			Christ.
Claire	331995	30/3	Latin. Bright, shining
First vowel A – to lead			girl.
Clare	33195	21/3	Latin. Bright shining
First vowel A – to lead			girl.
Colleen	3633555	30/3	Gaelic. Young girl.
First vowel O – to study			
Corissa	3699111	30/3	Latin/Greek. Most
First vowel O – to study			modest maiden.
Daphne	417855	30/3	Greek. Bay tree. A
First vowel A – to lead			symbol of victory.
Demetria	45452991	39/3	Greek. Fertility
First vowel E – to communicate			goddess.
Donna	46551	21/3	Italian. Noble lady.
First vowel O – to study			
Ella	5331	12/3	Teutonic. Beautiful,
First vowel E – to communicate			fiery.
Ellen	53355	21/3	Greek (Helen). Light.
First vowel E – to communicate			
Elrica	539931	30/3	Teutonic. Ruler of all.
First vowel E – to communicate			
Enyd	5574	21/3	Celtic. Purity of the
First vowel E – to communicate			soul.
Esther	512859	30/3	Hebrew. The star.
First vowel E – to communicate			
Eunice	535935	30/3	Greek. Happy and
First vowel E – to communicate			victorious.

Name	Number	Total	Origins and Meanings
Evita First vowel E – to communicate	54921	21/3	Hebrew. Life giver.
Evonne First vowel E – to communicate	546555	30/3	French. Archer with the yew bow.
Fifi First vowel I – intuition	6969	30/3	Hebrew (Josephine). She shall add.
Frances First vowel A – to lead	6915351	30/3	Latin. Free.
Gemma First vowel E – to communicate	75441	21/3	Latin. Precious stone.
Geralda First vowel E – to communicate	7591341	30/3	Teutonic. Noble spear carrier.
Geraldine First vowel E – to communicate	759134955	48/3	Teutonic. Noble spear carrier.
Griselda First vowel I – intuition	79915341	39/3	Teutonic. Grey heroine.
Gwyneth First vowel E – to communicate	7575528	39/3	Welsh. Blessed.
Helma First vowel E – to communicate	85341	21/3	Teutonic. Helmet.
Hester First vowel E – to communicate	851259	30/3	Hebrew (Esther). The star.
Hiberna First vowel I – intuition	8925951	39/3	Latin. Girl from Ireland.
Ianthe First vowel I – intuition	915285	30/3	Greek. Violet coloured flower.
Iona First vowel I – intuition	9651	21/3	Greek. Violet-coloured stone.
Isabel First vowel I – intuition	911253	21/3	Hebrew. Spanish form of Elizabeth.
Ita First vowel I – intuition	921	12/3	Gaelic. Desire for truth.
Jane First vowel A – to lead	1155	12/3	Hebrew. God's gift of grace.
Janette First vowel A – to lead	1155225	21/3	Hebrew. God's gift of grace.

Jasmin 111495 21/3
First vowel A – to lead
Arabic/Persian. Fragrant flower.

Jean 1515 12/3
First vowel E – to communicate
Hebrew. God's gift of grace.

Jessica 1511931 21/3
First vowel E – to communicate
Hebrew. The rich one.

Jinx 1956 21/3
First vowel I – intuition
Latin. Charming spell.

Julie 13395 21/3
First vowel U – to protect
Greek. Youthful.

Kirsty 299127 30/3
First vowel I – intuition
Norse. The annointed one.

Leila 35931 21/3
First vowel E – to communicate
Arabic. Black as the night.

Lilian 393915 30/3
First vowel I – intuition
Latin. A lily, pure.

Lindsay 3954117 30/3
First vowel I – intuition
Anglo-Saxon. Pool island.

Linsey 395157 30/3
First vowel I – intuition
Anglo-Saxon. Pool island.

Lunetta 3358221 21/3
First vowel U – to protect
Latin. Little Moon.

Madge 41475 21/3
First vowel A – to lead
Latin (Margaret). A pearl.

Magdala 4174131 21/3
First vowel A – to lead
Latin. A pearl.

Margareta 419719521 39/3
First vowel A – to lead
Latin. A pearl.

Marianne 41991555 39/3
First vowel A – to lead
Hebrew. Bitter and graceful.

Mary 4197 21/3
First vowel A – to lead
Hebrew. Bitterness.

Maud 4134 12/3
First vowel A – to lead
Teutonic. Brave little maid.

Maxine 416955 30/3
First vowel A – to lead
French. The greatest.

May 417 12/3
First vowel A – to lead
Latin. Born in May.

Name	Number	Total	Origins and Meanings
Myra	4791	21/3	Latin. Admired.
First vowel A – to lead			
Myrtle	479235	30/3	Greek. Victorious
First vowel E – to communicate			crown.
Nancy	51537	21/3	Hebrew (Anne). Full of
First vowel A – to lead			grace.
Neoma	55641	21/3	Greek. New Moon.
First vowel E – to communicate			
Ninon	59565	30/3	Hebrew (Anne). Full of
First vowel I – intuition			Grace.
Nora	5691	21/3	Greek (Helen). Light.
First vowel O – to study			
Ona	651	12/3	Latin. One.
First vowel O – to study			
Ophelia	6785391	39/3	Greek. Wise and
First vowel O – to study			immortal.
Orenda	695541	30/3	American Indian.
First vowel O – to study			Magical power.
Pamela	714531	21/3	Greek. All sweetness
First vowel A – to lead			and honey.
Pansy	71517	21/3	Greek. Flowerlike.
First vowel A – to lead			
Petula	752331	21/3	Greek. Steadfast as a
First vowel E – to communicate			rock. Fem. of Peter.
Philomena	789364551	48/3	Greek. Lover of the
First vowel I – intuition			Moon.
Querida	8359941	39/3	Spanish. Beloved one.
First vowel U – to protect			
Rachael	9138153	30/3	Hebrew. Innocent as a
First vowel A – to lead			lamb.
Rasia	91191	21/3	Greek (Rose). Beautiful
First vowel A – to lead			flower.
Rita	9921	21/3	Latin (Margaret). A
First vowel I – intuition			pearl.
Rohana	968151	30/3	Hindu. Sandalwood,
First vowel O – to study			sweet incense.

Rona 9651 21/3 Gaelic. A seal.
First vowel O – to study

Rosaline 96113955 39/3 Latin. Fair and beautiful
First vowel O – to study rose.

Rose 9615 21/3 Greek. Beautiful flower.
First vowel O – to study

Ruby 9327 21/3 Latin. Precious red
First vowel U – to protect jewel.

Sandra 115491 21/3 Greek (Alexandra).
First vowel A – to lead Helper of mankind.

Savina 114951 21/3 Latin (Sabina). Woman
First vowel A – to lead of the Sabine tribe.

Sharon 181965 30/3 Hebrew. Princess of
First vowel A – to lead exotic beauty.

Sherry 185997 39/3 Hebrew. Princess of
First vowel E – to communicate exotic beauty.

Sibylle 1927335 30/3 Greek. Prophetess.
First vowel I – intuition

Simone 194655 30/3 Hebrew. Heard by the
First vowel I – intuition Lord.

Sirena 199551 30/3 Greek. Sweet singing
First vowel I – intuition mermaid.

Tullia 233391 21/3 Gaelic. Peaceful one.
First vowel U – to protect

Verona 459651 30/3 Latin. Lady of Verona.
First vowel E – to communicate

Voleta 463521 21/3 French. Floating veil.
First vowel O – to study

Yedda 75441 21/3 Anglo-Saxon. The
First vowel E – to communicate singer.

Zelda 85341 21/3 Teutonic (Griselda).
First vowel E – to communicate Grey heroine.

NUMBER THREE NAMES –
BOYS

Name	Number	Total	Origins and Meanings
Alec First vowel A – to lead	1353	12/3	Greek. Derived from Alexander, 'helper and protector of mankind.'
Alexander First vowel A – to lead	135615459	39/3	Greek. Helper and protector of mankind.
Alister First vowel A – to lead	1391259	30/3	Greek. Helper and protector of mankind.
Allard First vowel A – to lead	133194	21/3	Anglo-Saxon. Noble and brave.
Alun First vowel A – to lead	1335	12/3	Gaelic. Cheerful harmony.
Amos First vowel A – to lead	1461	12/3	Hebrew. One who tackles difficulty.
Argus First vowel A – to lead	19731	21/3	Greek. Watchful one.
Aswin First vowel A – to lead	11595	21/3	Anglo-Saxon. Spear comrade
Augustus First vowel A – to lead	13731231	21/3	Latin. Exalted one.
Austin First vowel A – to lead	131295	21/3	Latin (Augustus). Exalted one.
Beagan First vowel E – to communicate	251715	21/3	Gaelic. Little one.
Ben First vowel E – to communicate	255	12/3	Hebrew. Shortened form of Benjamin, 'Son of my right hand'.
Bevis First vowel E – to communicate	25491	21/3	French. Fair view.
Blaise First vowel A – to lead	231915	21/3	Latin. Firebrand.

Blase 23115   12/3   Latin. Firebrand.
First vowel A – to lead

Brand 29154   21/3   Anglo-Saxon.
First vowel A – to lead   Firebrand.

Brien 29955   30/3   Celtic. Powerful
First vowel I – intuition   strength with virtue and honour.

Brooke 296625   30/3   Anglo-Saxon. One who
First vowel O – to study   lives by the brook.

Burke 23925   21/3   French. From the
First vowel U – to protect   stronghold.

Carlin 319395   30/3   Gaelic. Little champion.
First vowel A – to lead

Charles 3819351   30/3   Teutonic. The strong
First vowel A – to lead   man.

Colby 36327   21/3   Norse. From the dark
First vowel O – to study   country.

Conall 365133   21/3   Celtic. High and
First vowel O – to study   mighty.

Dermot 459462   30/3   Gaelic. Free man.
First vowel E – to communicate

Deryck 459732   30/3   Teutonic. Ruler of the
First vowel E – to communicate   people.

Devlin 454395   30/3   Gaelic. Fierce bravery.
First vowel E – to communicate

Dillon 493365   30/3   Gaelic. Faithful and
First vowel I – intuition   true.

Drake 49125   21/3   Anglo-Saxon. Dragon.
First vowel A – to lead

Duncan 435315   21/3   Celtic. Brown warrior.
First vowel U – to protect

Dunstan 4351215   21/3   Anglo-Saxon. From
First vowel U – to protect   brown stone hill.

Eamon 51465   21/3   Anglo-Saxon. Rich
First vowel E – to communicate   guardian.

Edric 54993   30/3   Anglo-Saxon. Fortune
First vowel E – to communicate   ruler.

Name	Number	Total	Origins and Meanings
Ellis First vowel E – to communicate	53391	21/3	Hebrew (Elias). The Lord is God.
Elroy First vowel E – to communicate	53967	30/3	French. The king.
Elton First vowel E – to communicate	53265	21/3	Anglo-Saxon. From the old farm.
Emery First vowel E – to communicate	54597	30/3	Teutonic. Industrious ruler.
Emil First vowel E – to communicate	5493	21/3	Teutonic. Industrious.
Emmanuel First vowel E – to communicate	54415353	30/3	Hebrew. 'God is with us.'
Eugene First vowel E – to communicate	537555	30/3	Greek. Nobly born.
Ferdinand First vowel E – to communicate	659495154	48/3	Teutonic. Bold adventurer.
Frewin First vowel E – to communicate	695595	39/3	Anglo-Saxon. Free, noble friend.
Galen First vowel A – to lead	71355	21/3	Gaelic. Little bright one.
George First vowel E – to communicate	756975	39/3	Greek. The farmer.
Goldwin First vowel O – to study	7634595	39/3	Anglo-Saxon. Son of the gold one.
Graham First vowel A – to lead	791814	30/3	Teutonic. From the grey lands.
Gunther First vowel U – to protect	7352859	39/3	Teutonic. Bold warrior.
Harrison First vowel A – to lead	81999165	48/3	Anglo-Saxon. Harold's son.
Herald First vowel E – to communicate	859134	30/3	Anglo-Saxon (Harold). Army commander.
Hollis First vowel O – to study	863391	30/3	Anglo-Saxon. Dweller in a holly grove.
Howell First vowel O – to study	865533	30/3	Celtic. Little, alert one.

Izaak 98112	21/3	Hebrew. The laughing one.
First vowel I – intuition		
James 11451	12/3	Hebrew (Jacob). The supplanter.
First vowel A – to lead		
Jarman 119415	21/3	Teutonic. The German.
First vowel A – to lead		
Jeffrey 1566957	39/3	Teutonic. God's divine peace.
First vowel E – to communicate		
Jerome 159645	30/3	Latin. Sacred, holy.
First vowel E – to communicate		
Jocelyn 1635375	30/3	Latin. Fair and just (a form of Justin).
First vowel O – to study		
Jock 1632	12/3	Hebrew (John/Jacob). God's gracious gift, the supplanter.
First vowel O – to study		
Jonah 16518	21/3	Hebrew. Peace.
First vowel O – to study		
Justin 131295	21/3	Latin. The just one.
First vowel U – to protect		
Kaspar 211719	21/3	Persian. Master of the treasure.
First vowel A – to lead		
Kingsley 29571357	39/3	Anglo-Saxon. From the King's meadow.
First vowel I – intuition		
Laurie 313995	30/3	Latin. Crowned with laurels.
First vowel A – to lead		
Leroy 35967	30/3	French. The king.
First vowel E – to communicate		
Levi 3549	21/3	Hebrew. United.
First vowel E – to communicate		
Linus 39531	21/3	Greek. Flame coloured hair.
First vowel I – intuition		
Luther 332859	30/3	Teutonic. Famous warrior.
First vowel U – to protect		
McDonald 43465134	30/3	Celtic. Son of Donald.
First vowel O – to study		
Magnus 417531	21/3	Latin. The great one.
First vowel A – to lead		

Name	Number	Total	Origins and Meanings
Manuel First vowel A – to lead	415353	21/3	Hebrew. Derived from Emmanuel, 'God is with us'.
Marcus First vowel A – to lead	419331	21/3	Latin. Follower of Mars.
Martin First vowel A – to lead	419295	30/3	Latin. Warlike person, Mars follower.
Mel First vowel E – to communicate	453	12/3	Celtic. Derived from Melvin.
Melvin First vowel E – to communicate	453495	30/3	Celtic (Malvin). Polished chief.
Meyer First vowel E – to communicate	45759	30/3	Teutonic. Steward.
Moss First vowel O – to study	4611	12/3	Hebrew. Derived from Moses, 'saved from the water'.
Nahum First vowel A – to lead	51834	21/3	Hebrew. Consoling.
Nathaniel First vowel A – to lead	512815953	39/3	Hebrew. Gift of God.
Niall First vowel I – intuition	59133	21/3	Gaelic. The champion.
Norman First vowel O – to study	569415	30/3	French. Man from the North.
Norward First vowel O – to study	5695194	39/3	Anglo-Saxon. Guardian from the North.
Orville First vowel O – to study	6949335	39/3	French. From the Golden Town.
Owen First vowel O – to study	6555	21/3	Celtic. Young, well-born warrior.
Pearce First vowel E – to communicate	751935	30/3	Latin (Peter). The rock.
Quinn First vowel U – to protect	83955	30/3	Gaelic. Wise and intelligent.
Reynold First vowel E – to communicate	9575634	39/3	Teutonic. Powerful ruler.

Roan 9615 21/3 Anglo-Saxon. From the
First vowel O – to study rowan tree.

Romeo 96456 30/3 Latin. Man from Rome.
First vowel O – to study

Roscoe 961365 30/3 Scandinavian. From the
First vowel O – to study deer forest.

Royce 96735 30/3 Anglo-Saxon. Son of a
First vowel O – to study king.

Rush 9318 21/3 French. Red-haired.
First vowel U – to protect

Sean 1515 12/3 Irish version of John.
First vowel E – to communicate God's gracious gift.

Silvester 193451259 39/3 Latin. From the forest.
First vowel I – intuition

Simeon 194565 30/3 Hebrew. One who
First vowel I – intuition hears.

Swain 15195 21/3 Anglo-Saxon. A
First vowel A – to lead herdsman.

Terrance 25991535 39/3 Latin. Smooth,
First vowel E – to communicate polished and tender.

Thaine 281955 30/3 Anglo-Saxon. Warrior's
First vowel A – to lead attendant.

Tobias 262911 21/3 Hebrew. 'God is good'.
First vowel O – to study

Uriah 39918 30/3 Hebrew. 'The Lord is
First vowel U – to protect my light'.

Valentine 413552955 39/3 Latin. Healthy and
First vowel A – to lead strong.

Vinson 495165 30/3 Anglo-Saxon. Son of
First vowel I – intuition Vincent.

Vito 4926 21/3 Latin. Alive and vital.
First vowel I – intuition

Willis 593391 30/3 Teutonic. Determined
First vowel I – intuition protector.

Wilton 593265 30/3 Anglo-Saxon. From the
First vowel I – intuition farm by the well.

NUMBER FOUR QUALITIES

If your number as a birth vibration is a Four you have been given the ability to build, plan, consolidate and make secure both your own life and that of your fellow man. Four is the number of the constructive builder, the foundation of the society that we all must exist within.

Four as a base number instils in those born with it the desire to make constructive use of what they may have at their disposal, be it on a lesser scale of family resources, or on a larger scale of our world's natural resources. It is called the number of the builder as it takes the ideas projected or thought of by others and puts them into practical use. A deep inner need for stability causes Fours to build strong houses, businesses and institutions for their own peace of mind and the stability of their fellow men.

Many Fours are to be found active in politics, banking and commerce as these are the larger foundations of the countries they live in.

Negative Fours lack the responsibility for their own actions and well-being. Always looking for someone else to take the blame when things go wrong.

Fours get on best with other Fours, Ones or Eights.

Any number of this vibration will strengthen the birth number and your child's personality. Or choose one of the three directional numbers (pp. 7–8).

TYPES OF FOURS

13/4 is a blend of leadership and communication; those of you with this type of base Four will strive to establish your own stability without need for support, direction or assistance from others. This type of Four can be too independent, neither accepting nor wanting criticism from others and apt to be a law unto himself.

22/4 See Master Numbers, pp. 142–3.

31/4 This Four tends to think and discuss what he is about to do before he actually does anything. This type of Four may have artistic inclinations and can be involved in the world of artistic commerce. The number can, though, be hesitant and is apt at times to change his mind.

40/4 The straight Four has only one real objective in life and that is to consolidate what he has achieved or has in his possession before moving on to the next rung of the ladder. Straight Fours are usually direct and to the point and will soon let you know if you threaten their security. Though a little too outspoken at times, a straight Four is only really defending what he fears may be threatened by change.

49/4 is a little bit more adventurous than most Fours and is even prepared to take limited risks in order to build his castles.

58/4 is a rare occurrence in single names but it does give the ability to communicate its owner's real feelings, which most other Fours lack.

67/4 Such Fours combine independence with a tendency to daydream. They like to do things their own way but, at the same time, have a basic need for security and stability. While often settling for safe, responsible careers involving little artistic talent, such Fours will indulge their imaginative qualities in artistic pastimes.

NUMBER FOUR NAMES – GIRLS

Name	Number	Total	Origins and Meanings
Angeline First vowel A – to lead	15753955	40/4	Greek. Heavenly messenger.
Aurelia First vowel U – to protect	1395391	31/4	Latin. Golden, the girl of the dawn.
Averil First vowel A – to lead	145993	31/4	Old English. Slayer of the boar.
Bena First vowel E – to communicate	2551	13/4	Hebrew. The wise one.
Bernadette First vowel E – to communicate	2595145225	40/4	French. Brave as the bear.
Beverley First vowel E – to communicate	25459357	40/4	Anglo-Saxon. The ambitious one.
Billie First vowel I – intuition	293395	31/4	Teutonic. Wise, resolute ruler.
Brucie First vowel U – to protect	293395	31/4	French. From the thicket.
Brunella First vowel U – to protect	29355331	31/4	Italian. One with brown hair.
Clarabella First vowel A – to lead	3319125331	31/4	Latin/French. Bright shining beauty.
Clorinda First vowel O – to study	33699541	40/4	Latin. Famed for her beauty.
Clotilda First vowel O – to study	33629341	31/4	Teutonic. Famous battle maiden.
Cordelia First vowel O – to study	36945391	40/4	Welsh. Jewel of the sea.
Constance First vowel O – to study	365121535	31/4	Latin. One who is constant.
Cytherea First vowel E – to communicate	37285951	40/4	Greek. From Cythera, another name for Aphrodite.
Darcie First vowel A – to lead	419395	31/4	French. From the fortress.

Elma	5341	13/4	Greek. Pleasant and amiable.
First vowel E – to communicate			
Elspeth	5317528	31/4	Hebrew. Consecrated to God.
First vowel E – to communicate			
Elva	5341	13/4	Anglo-Saxon. Friend of the elves.
First vowel E – to communicate			
Elvira	534991	31/4	Latin. White woman.
First vowel E – to communicate			
Emerald	5459134	31/4	French. The bright green jewel.
First vowel E – to communicate			
Emmeline	54453955	40/4	Teutonic. One who heals the universe.
First vowel E – to communicate			
Evangeline	5415753955	49/4	Greek. Bearer of glad tidings.
First vowel E – to communicate			
Fedora	654691	31/4	Greek (Theodora). Gift of God.
First vowel E – to communicate			
Genevieve	755549545	49/4	French. Pure white wave.
First vowel E – to communicate			
Georgina	75697951	49/4	Greek. Girl from the farm.
First vowel E – to communicate			
Godiva	764941	31/4	Anglo-Saxon. Gift of God.
First vowel O – to study			
Harmony	8194657	40/4	Latin. Concord and harmony.
First vowel A – to lead			
Hayley	817357	31/4	English. From place or field name.
First vowel A – to lead			
Honey	86557	31/4	English. Sweet one.
First vowel O – to study			
Ila	931	13/4	French. From the island.
First vowel I – intuition			
Isadora	9114691	31/4	Greek. The gift of Isis.
First vowel I – intuition			
Jeannette	151555225	31/4	Hebrew. God's gift of grace.
First vowel E – to communicate			
Jenifer	1559659	40/4	Celtic. White phantom.
First vowel E – to communicate			
Jillian	1933915	31/4	Latin. Young nestling.
First vowel I – intuition			

Name	Number	Total	Origins and Meanings
Joan 1615 First vowel O – to study		13/4	Hebrew (Jane). God's gracious gift.
Kathleen 21283555 First vowel A – to lead		31/4	Greek. Pure maiden.
Leala 35131 First vowel E – to communicate		13/4	French. The true one.
Leda 3541 First vowel E – to communicate		13/4	Greek. Mother of beauty.
Lee 355 First vowel E – to communicate		13/4	English. From the fields.
Lisabeth 39112528 First vowel I – intuition		31/4	Hebrew. Consecrated to God.
Lola 3631 First vowel O – to study		13/4	Spanish. Strong woman.
Lorelei 3695359 First vowel O – to study		40/4	Teutonic. Siren of the river.
Luana 33151 First vowel U – to protect		13/4	Teutonic. Graceful army maiden.
Lysandra 37115491 First vowel A – to lead		31/4	Greek. The liberator.
Magdalane 417413155 First vowel A – to lead		31/4	Greek. Tower of strength.
Malva 41341 First vowel A – to lead		13/4	Greek. Soft and tender.
Martina 4192951 First vowel A – to lead		31/4	Latin. Warlike one.
Melinda 4539541 First vowel E – to communicate		31/4	Greek. Mild and gentle, homely.
Mercia 459391 First vowel E – to communicate		31/4	Anglo-Saxon. Lady of Mercia, the old Saxon country.
Michelle 49385335 First vowel I – intuition		40/4	Hebrew. Likeness to God. Fem. of Michael.
Morwenna 46955551 First vowel O – to study		40/4	Cornish. A sea wave.
Nicole 593635 First vowel I – intuition		31/4	Greek. The leader of the people.

Oriana	699151	31/4	Latin. Golden one.
First vowel O – to study			
Persephone	7591578655	58/4	Greek. Goddess of the
First vowel E – to communicate			Underworld.
Psyche	717385	31/4	Greek. Of the soul and
First vowel E – to communicate			mind.
Queenie	8355595	40/4	Teutonic. The queen.
First vowel E – to communicate			
Rosemarie	961541995	49/4	Latin. Dew of the sea.
First vowel O – to study			
Rowena	965551	31/4	Anglo-Saxon. Friend
First vowel O – to study			with white hair.
Royale	967135	31/4	French. Regal being.
First vowel O – to study			
Tara	2191	13/4	Gaelic. Towering rock.
First vowel A – to lead			
Theone	285655	31/4	Greek. The name of
First vowel E – to communicate			God.
Theresa	2859511	31/4	Greek. The harvester.
First vowel E – to communicate			
Tomasine	26411953	31/4	Hebrew. The twin. Fem.
First vowel O – to study			of Thomas.
Trixie	299695	40/4	Latin (Beatrice). She
First vowel I – intuition			who brings joy.
Valda	41341	13/4	Teutonic. The ruler.
First vowel A – to lead			
Venetia	4555291	31/4	Latin. Lady of Venice.
First vowel E – to communicate			
Vesta	45121	13/4	Latin. Guardian of the
First vowel E – to communicate			sacred flame.
Winona	595651	31/4	American Indian. First
First vowel I – intuition			born daughter.
Zerlina	8593951	40/4	Teutonic. Serene
First vowel E – to communicate			beauty.

Note: Refer to the section on Master Numbers 22 for Girls
(pp. 146–8) for a further selection of Four names.

NUMBER FOUR NAMES – BOYS

Name	Number	Total	Origins and Meanings
Adriel First vowel A – to lead	149953	31/4	Hebrew. From God's congregation.
Allan First vowel A – to lead	13315	13/4	Gaelic. Cheerful harmony.
Archibald First vowel A – to lead	193892134	40/4	Teutonic. Nobly and truly bold.
Auberon First vowel A – to lead	1325965	31/4	Teutonic. Elf ruler.
Baldric First vowel A – to lead	2134993	31/4	Teutonic. Princely ruler.
Blake First vowel A – to lead	23125	13/4	Anglo-Saxon. Of fair complexion.
Borden First vowel O – to study	269455	31/4	Anglo-Saxon. From the valley of the boar.
Bradley First vowel A – to lead	2914357	31/4	Anglo-Saxon. From the broad meadow.
Brendan First vowel E – to communicate	2955415	31/4	Gaelic. Little raven, or from the fairy hill.
Broderick First vowel O – to study	296459932	49/4	Anglo-Saxon. From the broad ridge.
Budd First vowel U – to protect	2344	13/4	Anglo-Saxon. Herald, the bringer of news.
Burney First vowel U – to protect	239557	31/4	Anglo-Saxon. Dwells on the island in the brook.
Christopher First vowel I – intuition	38991267859	67/4	French. A Christian.
Churchill First vowel U – to protect	383938933	49/4	Anglo-Saxon. Lives by the church on the hill.
Cornel First vowel O – to study	369553	31/4	Latin. Battle horn.
Courtney First vowel O – to study	36392557	40/4	French. A place.
Cyrano First vowel A – to lead	379156	31/4	Greek. Man from Cyprus.

Cyril   37993   31/4   Greek. The lord.
First vowel I – intuition

Dale   4135   13/4   Teutonic. Dweller in the
First vowel A – to lead   valley.

Dallas   413311   13/4   Celtic. Skilled, or from
First vowel A – to lead   the water field.

Dexter   456259   31/4   Latin: The right-handed
First vowel E – to communicate   man.

Diggory   4977697   49/4   Anglo-Saxon. Strayed
First vowel I – intuition   and found.

Dominic   4649593   40/4   Latin. Belonging to the
First vowel O – to study   Lord, born on Sunday.

Emory   54697   31/4   Teutonic (Emery).
First vowel E – to communicate   Industrious ruler.

Ewing   55957   31/4   Anglo-Saxon. Friend of
First vowel E – to communicate   the law.

Falkner   6132559   31/4   Anglo-Saxon. Falcon
First vowel A – to lead   trainer.

Fergus   659731   31/4   Gaelic. The raven,
First vowel E – to communicate   symbol of wisdom.

Finlay   695317   31/4   Gaelic. Fair soldier.
First vowel I – intuition

Franklin   69152395   40/4   Anglo-Saxon.
First vowel A – to lead   Freeholder of property.

Fraser   691159   31/4   French. Strawberry, or
First vowel A – to lead   curly haired.

Garard   719194   31/4   Anglo-Saxon. Mighty
First vowel A – to lead   spear warrior.

Garrard   7199194   40/4   Anglo-Saxon. Mighty
First vowel A – to lead   spear warrior.

Garrick   7199932   40/4   Anglo-Saxon. Spear
First vowel A – to lead   ruler.

Graeme   791545   31/4   Teutonic. From the
First vowel A – to lead   grey lands.

Grover   796459   40/4   Anglo-Saxon. One who
First vowel O – to study   comes from the grove.

Hamish   814918   31/4   Hebrew (James). The
First vowel A – to lead   supplanter.

Name	Number	Total	Origins and Meanings
Harold First vowel A – to lead	819634	31/4	Anglo-Saxon. Army commander.
Hiram First vowel I – intuition	89914	31/4	Hebrew. Most noble and exalted.
Jacob First vowel A – to lead	11362	13/4	Hebrew. The supplanter.
Jeremy First vowel E – to communicate	159547	31/4	Hebrew. Exalted by the Lord.
Jesse First vowel E – to communicate	15115	13/4	Hebrew. God's gift.
Jethro First vowel E – to communicate	152896	31/4	Hebrew. Exalted without equal.
Jules First vowel U – to protect	13351	13/4	Latin. Youthful.
Kane First vowel A – to lead	2155	13/4	Celtic. Little warrior, or radiant brightness.
Kenith First vowel E – to communicate	255928	31/4	Celtic. Handsome.
Kennard First vowel E – to communicate	2555194	31/4	Anglo-Saxon. Bold and vigorous.
Kermit First vowel E – to communicate	259492	31/4	Celtic. A free man.
Kieran First vowel I – intuition	295915	31/4	Gaelic. Small and dark skinned.
Lee First vowel E – to communicate	355	13/4	Anglo-Saxon/Gaelic. From the meadow, or poetic.
Linden First vowel I – intuition	395455	31/4	Anglo-Saxon. From the lime tree.
Lionel First vowel I – intuition	396553	31/4	French. The young lion.
Ludwig First vowel U – to protect	334597	31/4	Teutonic (Lewis). Famous battle warrior.
Luke First vowel U – to protect	3325	13/4	Latin (Lucius). Light.
Merritt First vowel E – to communicate	4599922	40/4	French. Little famous one.

Name	Number		Meaning
Nixon 59665 First vowel I – intuition		31/4	Anglo-Saxon. Nicholas's son.
Obadiah 6214918 First vowel O – to study		31/4	Hebrew. Servant of the Lord.
Patric 712993 First vowel A – to lead		31/4	Latin. One of noble birth.
Piers 79591 First vowel I – intuition		31/4	French form of Peter, 'the rock'.
Renny 95557 First vowel E – to communicate		31/4	Gaelic. Little, mighty and powerful.
Robin 96295 First vowel O – to study		31/4	Teutonic (Robert). Bright, shining fame.
Rodger 964759 First vowel O – to study		40/4	Teutonic. Famous spearman.
Rory 9697 First vowel O – to study		31/4	Gaelic. Red king.
Rudolph 9346378 First vowel U – to protect		40/4	Teutonic. Famous wolf.
Sidney 194557 First vowel I – intuition		31/4	French. A follower of St. Denis.
Sinclair 19533199 First vowel I – intuition		40/4	French. From St. Clare.
Solomon 1636465 First vowel O – to study		31/4	Hebrew. Wise and peaceful.
Theobald 28562134 First vowel E – to communicate		31/4	Teutonic. Bold leader of the people.
Torrance 26991535 First vowel O – to study		40/4	Gaelic. From the little hills.
Travers 2914591 First vowel A – to lead		31/4	Latin. From the crossroads.
Washington 5118957265 First vowel A – to lead		49/4	Anglo-Saxon. From the keen-eyed one's farm.
Wilbur 593239 First vowel I – intuition		31/4	Teutonic. Resolute and brilliant.

Note: Refer to the section on Master Numbers 22 for Boys (pp. 149–52) for a further selection of Four names.

NUMBER FIVE QUALITIES

If your birth number reduces to a five you are adventurous, communicative and freedom seeking. You can adapt to the environment you are in, and yet are always seeking change. Five is the number of the explorer. There is something about this vibration that defies society as we know it. Fives have enquiring minds and need to know why things are, rather than being able merely to accept them.

Fives tend to be a little impatient, as their need to seek the truth or the reason for things can bring them into conflict with the masses who need security. In the old West the explorers and pioneers were the Fives, always needing to move on and explore more as the budding Fours arrived to build towns in what was wild.

A quick sharp mind can be matched by a short sharp tongue and many Fives say exactly what they feel, which does not always go down well with others.

The best matches for Fives are with other Fives, Twos and Sevens.

Any number of this vibration will strengthen the birth number and your child's personality. Or choose one of the three directional numbers (pp. 7–8).

TYPES OF FIVES

14/5   confers leadership and a degree of stability to a Five. It allows him more readily to accept responsibility for his actions, words or deeds.

23/5   is a more sedate type when at home or at rest. Just as boisterous and adventurous to external appearances but with an inner need to build a safe haven to retreat to for periods of rest and recuperation.

32/5   is a reversal of the 23/5. These Fives may form partnerships or associations far from the place of birth. They need to enjoy life to the full before settling down to become the steady bringer of law and stability to their chosen environment. Quite a physical Five.

41/4   is the type that would be well placed in military, governmental or social work. The desire is to make everyone as safe and secure as possible, for in so doing he finds the security and praise he requires. This Five is a fighter.

50/5   Straight Fives are blunt and to the point. Others may find them at times insensitive but it is only their outer shell which applies logic to the problem in hand that would make you think so. This type of Five is, in fact, very sensitive to the needs of his fellow man.

59/5   has been everywhere, done everything and seen all he ever desired to see before he realises that he must build a more secure base to retire to. He has no regrets, spends what he earns and enjoys life to the full, but God help you if you ever get on his wrong side as the combination of mental and physical makes him a very bad enemy.

NUMBER FIVE NAMES – GIRLS

Name	Number	Total	Origins and Meanings
Abigail First vowel A – to lead	1297193	32/5	Hebrew. Father rejoiced.
Adah First vowel A – to lead	1418	14/5	Hebrew. The crown's adornment.
Adela First vowel A – to lead	14531	14/5	Teutonic. Noble and kind.
Adelaide First vowel A – to lead	14531945	32/5	Teutonic. Noble and kind.
Adeline First vowel A – to lead	1453955	32/5	Teutonic. Noble and kind.
Alberta First vowel A – to lead	1325921	23/5	Teutonic. Noble and brilliant.
Alfonsine First vowel A – to lead	136651955	41/5	Teutonic. Noble and ready.
Alphonsia First vowel A – to lead	137865191	41/5	Teutonic. Noble and ready.
Alvina First vowel A – to lead	134951	23/5	Teutonic. Noble and loved friend.
Alyssa First vowel A – to lead	137111	14/5	Greek. Sane one.
Amelia First vowel A – to lead	145391	23/5	Teutonic. Industrious and striving.
Amelinda First vowel A – to lead	14539541	32/5	Spanish. Beloved and pretty.
Bab First vowel A – to lead	212	5	Arabic. From the gateway.
Bella First vowel E – to communicate	25331	14/5	French. Beautiful woman.
Blodwyn First vowel O – to study	2364575	32/5	Welsh. White flower.
Blossom First vowel O – to study	2361164	23/5	Old English. Fragrant as a flower.

Caitlin 3192395 32/5 Greek. Pure maiden.
First vowel A – to lead

Cara 3191 14/5 Celtic, friend. Or
First vowel A – to lead Italian, dearest one.

Caroline 31963955 41/5 Teutonic. Little woman
First vowel A – to lead born to command.

Cherry 385997 41/5 French. Dear one.
First vowel E – to communicate

Cladogh 3314678 32/5 Gaelic. A river in
First vowel A – to lead Tipperary.

Cornelia 36955391 41/5 Latin. Womanly virtue.
First vowel O – to study

Danica 415931 23/5 Norse. Morning star.
First vowel A – to lead

Darlene 4193555 32/5 Anglo-Saxon. Little
First vowel A – to lead darling.

Dee 455 14/5 Welsh. Dark beauty.
First vowel E – to communicate

Deva 4541 14/5 Sanskrit. Divine, the
First vowel E – to communicate Moon goddess.

Dido 4946 23/5 Greek. Teacher.
First vowel I – intuition

Dominica 46495931 41/5 Latin. Belonging to the
First vowel O – to study Lord.

Dorothea 46962851 41/5 Greek. Gift of God.
First vowel O – to study

Duana 43151 14/5 Gaelic. Little dark
First vowel U – to protect maiden.

Easter 511259 23/5 Old English. Born at
First vowel E – to communicate Easter.

Eileen 593555 32/5 Celtic (Helen). Light.
First vowel E – to communicate

Elise 53915 23/5 Hebrew (Elizabeth).
First vowel E – to communicate Consecrated to God.

Elna 5351 14/5 Greek (Helen). Light.
First vowel E – to communicate

Elsie 53195 23/5 Hebrew (Elizabeth).
First vowel E – to communicate Consecrated to God.

Name	Number	Total	Origins and Meanings
Emma First vowel E – to communicate	5441	14/5	Teutonic. One who heals the Universe.
Enrica First vowel E – to communicate	559931	32/5	Italian form of Henrietta.
Ethel First vowel E – to communicate	52853	23/5	Teutonic. Noble maiden.
Eve First vowel E – to communicate	545	14/5	Hebrew. Life giver.
Evelina First vowel E – to communicate	5453951	32/5	Hebrew. Life giver.
Fay First vowel A – to lead	617	14/5	French, a fairy. Or Irish, a raven.
Fayme First vowel A – to lead	61745	23/5	French. Of high reputation.
Filma First vowel I – intuition	69341	23/5	Anglo-Saxon. Misty veil, beauty.
Gaea First vowel A – to lead	7151	14/5	Greek. The Earth.
Gayle First vowel A – to lead	71735	23/5	Hebrew (Abigail). 'Father rejoiced'.
Georgiana First vowel E – to communicate	756979151	50/5	Greek. Fem. of George, 'the farmer'.
Gladys First vowel A – to lead	731471	23/5	Celtic. Frail, delicate flower.
Glynis First vowel I – intuition	737591	32/5	Celtic. From the valley.
Hylda First vowel A – to lead	87341	23/5	Teutonic. Battle maid.
Ida First vowel I – intuition	941	14/5	Teutonic. Happy.
Imogene First vowel I – intuition	9467555	41/5	Latin. Image of her mother.
Irma First vowel I – intuition	9941	23/5	Latin. Noble person.
Iva First vowel I – intuition	941	14/5	French. The yew tree.

Janet	11552	14/5	Hebrew. God's gift of grace.
First vowel A – to lead			
Janthina	11528951	32/5	Greek. Violet coloured flower.
First vowel A – to lead			
Jessamine	15111955	32/5	Persian. Fragrant flower.
First vowel E – to communicate			
Joanne	161555	23/5	Hebrew. God's gift of grace.
First vowel O – to study			
Josilyn	1619375	32/5	Latin. Fair and just. Fem. of Justin.
First vowel O – to study			
Jovita	164921	23/5	Latin. The joyful one.
First vowel O – to study			
Joy	167	14/5	Latin. Gay and joyful.
First vowel O – to study			
Juliet	133952	23/5	Greek. Youthful.
First vowel U – to protect			
June	1355	14/5	Latin. Summer child.
First vowel U – to protect			
Kerry	25997	32/5	Gaelic. Dark one.
First vowel E – to communicate			
Lara	3191	14/5	Latin. Famous.
First vowel A – to lead			
Laverne	3145955	32/5	French. Spring-like or alder tree.
First vowel A – to lead			
Lavinia	3149591	32/5	Latin. Lady of Rome.
First vowel A – to lead			
Lena	3551	14/5	Latin. Enchanting one.
First vowel E – to communicate			
Lisa	3911	14/5	Hebrew (Elizabeth). Consecrated to God.
First vowel I – intuition			
Louisa	363911	23/5	Teutonic. Famous battle maid.
First vowel O – to study			
Madeleine	4197195221	41/5	Greek. Tower of strength.
First vowel A – to lead			
Margaretta	4197195221	41/5	Latin. A pearl.
First vowel A – to lead			
Marguerita	4197359921	50/5	Latin. A pearl.
First vowel A – to lead			

Name	Number	Total	Origins and Meanings
Marlene First vowel A – to lead	4193555	32/5	Greek. Tower of strength.
Mathilda First vowel A – to lead	41289341	32/5	Teutonic. Brave little warrior.
Maureen First vowel A – to lead	4139555	32/5	Hebrew (Mary). Bitterness.
Melanie First vowel E – to communicate	4531595	32/5	Greek. Clad in darkness.
Merrie First vowel E – to communicate	459995	41/5	Anglo-Saxon. Mirthful, joyous.
Minette First vowel I – intuition	4955225	32/5	French. Little kitten.
Mira First vowel I – intuition	4991	23/5	Latin. Wonderful one.
Mitzi First vowel I – intuition	49289	32/5	Hebrew. (Mary). Bitterness.
Molly First vowel O – to study	46337	23/5	Hebrew. (Mary). Bitterness.
Morgan First vowel O – to study	469715	32/5	Welsh. White sea.
Nesta First vowel E – to communicate	55121	14/5	Greek (Agnes). Pure, chaste, lamblike.
Olivia First vowel O – to study	639491	32/5	Latin. The olive tree.
Patricia First vowel A – to lead	71299391	41/5	Latin. Well born maiden.
Posy First vowel O – to study	7817	23/5	English. Small bunch of flowers.
Prudence First vowel U – to protect	79345535	41/5	Latin. Cautious foresight.
Rachell First vowel A – to lead	9138533	32/5	Hebrew. Innocent as a lamb.
Renata First vowel E – to communicate	955121	23/5	Latin. Born again, reincarnated.
Robina First vowel O – to study	962951	32/5	Anglo-Saxon. Of shining fame.

Rosanne 9611555 32/5 English. Graceful rose.
First vowel O – to study

Sabine 112955 23/5 Latin. Woman of the
First vowel A – to lead Sabine tribe.

Samantha 11415281 23/5 Aramaic. A listener.
First vowel A – to lead

Sherri 185999 41/5 French (Cherie). Dear,
First vowel E – to communicate beloved one.

Shelley 1853357 32/5 English. From the edge
First vowel E – to communicate of the meadow.

Siobhan 1962815 32/5 Irish version of Jane,
First vowel I – intuition 'God's gift'.

Sofia 16691 23/5 Greek. Wisdom.
First vowel O – to study

Sonja 16511 14/5 Greek (Sophia).
First vowel O – to study Wisdom.

Sophia 167891 32/5 Greek. Wisdom.
First vowel O – to study

Stacy 12137 14/5 Greek (Anastasia). She
First vowel A – to lead who will rise again.

Teresa 259511 23/5 Greek. Harvester.
First vowel E – to communicate

Terry 25997 32/5 Greek (Teresa).
First vowel E – to communicate Harvester.

Thelma 285341 23/5 Greek. Nursling.
First vowel E – to communicate

Theodora 28564691 41/5 Greek. Gift of God.
First vowel E – to communicate

Thomasine 286411955 41/5 Hebrew. The twin. Fem.
First vowel O – to study of Thomas.

Velvet 453452 23/5 English. Soft as velvet.
First vowel E – to communicate

Vivian 494915 32/5 Latin. Alive, vivid or
First vowel I – intuition vibrant.

Yvonne 746555 32/5 French. The archer with
First vowel O – to study the yew bow.

Zillah 893318 32/5 Hebrew. Shadow.
First vowel I – intuition

NUMBER FIVE NAMES – BOYS

Name	Number	Total	Origins and Meanings
Alberic First vowel A – to lead	1325993	32/5	Teutonic. Elf ruler.
Aldo First vowel A – to lead	1346	14/5	Teutonic. Old, wise and rich.
Algernon First vowel A – to lead	13759565	41/5	French. The whiskered one.
Anatole First vowel A – to lead	1512635	23/5	Greek. From the East.
Arnaud First vowel A – to lead	195134	23/5	Teutonic. Strong as an eagle.
Arthur First vowel A – to lead	192839	32/5	Celtic. Noble bear man, strong.
Ashton First vowel A – to lead	118265	23/5	Anglo-Saxon. Dweller at the ash tree.
Bart First vowel A – to lead	2192	14/5	Hebrew. Shortened form of Bartholomew, 'the ploughman'.
Benjamin First vowel E – to communicate	25511495	32/5	Hebrew. Son of my right hand.
Benoni First vowel E – to communicate	255659	32/5	Hebrew. Son of my sorrow.
Bertram First vowel E – to communicate	2592914	32/5	Anglo-Saxon. Bright raven.
Bing First vowel I – intuition	2957	23/5	Teutonic. Kettle-shaped hollow.
Boyce First vowel O – to study	26735	23/5	French. From the woods.
Brandon First vowel A – to lead	2915465	32/5	Anglo-Saxon. From the beacon on the hill.
Brent First vowel E – to communicate	29552	23/5	Anglo-Saxon. Steep hill.
Caleb First vowel A – to lead	31352	14/5	Hebrew. The bold one.

Cecil 35393 23/5 Latin. The unseeing
First vowel E – to communicate one.

Claud 33134 14/5 Latin. The lame.
First vowel A – to lead

Clay 3317 14/5 Anglo-Saxon. From the
First vowel A – to lead claypit.

Conlan 365315 23/5 Gaelic. The hero.
First vowel O – to study

Courtenay 363925517 41/5 French. A place.
First vowel O – to study

Darby 41927 23/5 Gaelic. Freeman.
First vowel A – to lead

Davin 41495 23/5 Scandinavian.
First vowel A – to lead Brightness of the Finns.

Derick 459932 32/5 Teutonic. Ruler of the
First vowel E – to communicate people.

Derrick 4599932 41/5 Teutonic. Ruler of the
First vowel E – to communicate people.

Donahue 4651835 32/5 Gaelic. Warrior clad in
First vowel O – to study brown.

Donald 465134 23/5 Celtic. Ruler of the
First vowel O – to study world.

Drew 4955 23/5 Gaelic. The wise one.
First vowel E – to communicate

Drury 49397 32/5 French. The dear one.
First vowel U – to protect

Duke 4325 14/5 French. Leader.
First vowel U – to protect

Eachan 513815 23/5 Gaelic. Little horse.
First vowel E – to communicate

Earle 51935 23/5 Anglo-Saxon.
First vowel E – to communicate Nobleman, chief.

Eldon 53465 23/5 Teutonic. Respected
First vowel E – to communicate elder.

Eleazar 5351819 32/5 Hebrew. Helped by
First vowel E – to communicate God.

Ellison 5339165 32/5 Anglo-Saxon. Son of
First vowel E – to communicate Elias.

Name	Number	Total	Origins and Meanings
Errol	59963	32/5	Anglo-Saxon (Earl).
First vowel E – to communicate			Nobleman or chief.
Euan	5315	14/5	Gaelic. Well born young
First vowel E – to communicate			warrior.
Ezra	5891	23/5	Hebrew. The one who
First vowel E – to communicate			helps.
Fiske	69125	23/5	Anglo-Saxon. Fish.
First vowel I – intuition			
Fletcher	63523859	41/5	French. The arrow
First vowel E – to communicate			maker.
Frank	69152	23/5	Anglo-Saxon.
First vowel A – to lead			Freeholder of property.
Gervase	7594115	32/5	Teutonic. Spear vassal.
First vowel E – to communicate			
Gilroy	793967	41/5	Latin, the king's
First vowel I – intuition			servant. Gaelic, the
			red-haired one.
Gareth	719528	32/5	French/Welsh. From the
First vowel A – to lead			garden.
Gregory	7957697	50/5	Greek. The watchful
First vowel E – to communicate			one.
Gustave	7312145	23/5	Scandinavian. Staff of
First vowel U – to protect			the gods.
Gyles	77351	23/5	Latin. Shield bearer.
First vowel E – to communicate			
Hadwin	814595	32/5	Anglo-Saxon. Battle
First vowel A – to lead			companion.
Hamar	81419	23/5	Norse. Symbol of
First vowel A – to lead			ingenuity.
Hamlet	814352	23/5	Teutonic. Little village.
First vowel A – to lead			
Hammond	8144654	32/5	Teutonic. Small home
First vowel A – to lead			lover.
Herman	859415	32/5	Teutonic. Army warrior.
First vowel E – to communicate			
Homer	86459	32/5	Greek. Pledge.
First vowel O – to study			

Horace	869135	32/5	Latin. Time keeper.
First vowel O – to study			
Horatio	8691296	41/5	Latin. Time keeper.
First vowel O – to study			
Isaak	91112	14/5	Hebrew. The laughing one.
First vowel I – intuition			
Ivar	9419	23/5	Norse. Battle archer.
First vowel I – intuition			
Jason	11165	14/5	Greek. The healer.
First vowel A – to lead			
Joachim	1613894	32/5	Hebrew. Judgment of the Lord.
First vowel O – to study			
Jonas	16511	14/5	Hebrew. Man of the people.
First vowel O – to study			
Keenan	255515	23/5	Celtic. Little handsome one.
First vowel E – to communicate			
Kelsey	253157	23/5	Norse. Dweller on an island.
First vowel E – to communicate			
Kenneth	2555528	32/5	Celtic. Handsome or royal oath.
First vowel E – to communicate			
Kent	2552	14/5	Celtic. Bright and white.
First vowel E – to communicate			
Kerry	25997	32/5	Gaelic. Son of the dark one.
First vowel E – to communicate			
Killian	2933915	32/5	Gaelic. Little warlike one.
First vowel I – intuition			
Leander	3515459	32/5	Greek. The lion man.
First vowel E – to communicate			
Leigh	35978	32/5	Anglo-Saxon, from the meadow. Gaelic, poetic.
First vowel E – to communicate			
Lemuel	354353	23/5	Hebrew. Consecrated to God.
First vowel E – to communicate			
Leo	356	14/5	Latin. Lion.
First vowel E – to communicate			
Lewis	35591	23/5	Teutonic. Famous battle warrior.
First vowel E – to communicate			

Name	Number	Total	Origins and Meanings
Lindon	395465	32/5	Anglo-Saxon. From the lime tree.
First vowel I – intuition			
Lloyd	33674	23/5	Welsh. Grey-haired.
First vowel O – to study			
Ludovic	3346493	32/5	Latin form of Lewis.
First vowel U – to protect			
Marvin	419495	32/5	Anglo-Saxon. Famous friend.
First vowel A – to lead			
Medwin	454595	32/5	Anglo-Saxon. Powerful friend.
First vowel E – to communicate			
Meridith	45994928	50/5	Anglo-Saxon. Guardian from the sea.
First vowel E – to communicate			
Morgan	469715	32/5	Welsh. White sea, foam waves.
First vowel O – to study			
Neal	5513	14/5	Gaelic. The champion.
First vowel E – to communicate			
Ned	554	14/5	Anglo-Saxon (Edward). To prosper.
First vowel E – to communicate			
Niles	59351	23/5	Gaelic (Neal). The champion.
First vowel I – intuition			
Orval	69413	23/5	Anglo-Saxon. Mighty spear.
First vowel O – to study			
Paul	7133	14/5	Latin. Small.
First vowel A – to lead			
Percival	75939413	41/5	French. Valley piercer.
First vowel E – to communicate			
Quillan	8393315	32/5	Gaelic. Cub.
First vowel U – to protect			
Quintin	8395295	41/5	Latin. Fifth born son.
First vowel U – to protect			
Rad	914	14/5	Anglo-Saxon. Advisor, counsellor.
First vowel A – to lead			
Randal	915413	23/5	Old English. Shield wolf.
First vowel A – to lead			
Reed	9554	23/5	Anglo-Saxon. Red-haired.
First vowel E – to communicate			

Roald 96134 23/5 Teutonic. Famous
First vowel O – to study ruler.

Rodd 9644 23/5 Teutonic. Famous,
First vowel O – to study wealthy ruler.

Scott 13622 14/5 Latin/Celtic. From
First vowel O – to study Scotland/Tattooed
warrior.

Septimus 15729431 32/5 Latin. Seventh born
First vowel E – to communicate son.

Serle 15935 23/5 Teutonic. Bearer of
First vowel E – to communicate arms.

Shelley 1853357 32/5 Anglo-Saxon. From the
First vowel E – to communicate hill-ledge meadow.

Slade 13145 14/5 Anglo-Saxon. Valley
First vowel A – to lead dweller.

Stacy 12137 14/5 Greek (Eustace).
First vowel A – to lead Prosperous and stable.

Sterling 12593957 41/5 Teutonic, good,
First vowel E – to communicate honest. Celtic, from
the yellow house.

Tab 212 5 Teutonic. The
First vowel A – to lead drummer.

Trent 29552 23/5 Latin. The torrent.
First vowel E – to communicate

Vere 4595 23/5 Latin. Faithful and true.
First vowel E – to communicate

Virgil 499793 41/5 Latin. Staff bearer,
First vowel I – intuition strong.

Wayne 51755 23/5 Teutonic.
First vowel A – to lead Wagon-maker.

Wilfred 5936954 41/5 Teutonic. Firm peace
First vowel I – intuition maker.

Xerxes 659651 32/5 Persian. The king.
First vowel E – to communicate

NUMBER SIX QUALITIES

If your birth number reduces to one of the Six vibrations, you are artistic, refined, with a degree of vanity and a desire for reassurance. You may have green fingers, desire many children or want to share your feelings of love with all whom you come into contact with.

Six is the number of Venus, artistic sensitivity and a need to see justice and fair play for all. There can be a tendency to vanity and laziness, for if others fail to appreciate or recognise what a Six is doing, he tends to lose the interest and desire to do it.

Sixes are best expressed through the Arts, and creative spheres of life. The number needs to grow, expand and receive recognition in order that it may move on to its next task. Sixes of either sex are very loving and demand the same attention from their chosen mate. Many Sixes have large families as they have an abundance of love to give and can best find an outlet for it with children. Sixes can be petty and childish themselves if hurt or left with an empty feeling.

If you are a Six, your best matches are with other Sixes, Threes or Nines.

Any number of this vibration will strengthen the birth number and your child's personality. Or choose one of the three directional numbers (pp. 7–8).

TYPES OF SIXES

15/6   This type of Six has both the ability to lead and communicate his feelings, desires and ambitions to the general masses. Hard outer shell until you win his trust, but if you do, you have a true friend for life.

24/6   This type of Six is more concerned with the home (4) and partnership (2). He or she can be expressive and helpful to others but charity begins at home and they and theirs must be looked after first. House-proud with larger than average families.

33/6   See Master Numbers Section 33 (p. 143).

42/6   This type of Six can become involved with charities or large social issues. He or she tends to look on all of society as being brothers, sisters or children and would make an excellent arbitrator or social worker.

51/6   It is hard to tie down a 51/6. He is the most selfish of the Sixes and needs to learn by his own mistakes before settling down. The desire to have the world as a home and much travel can be associated with this vibration. He must learn to trust others more, though.

60/6   Too high as a name vibration.

NUMBER SIX NAMES – GIRLS

Name	Number	Total	Origins and Meanings
Ada First vowel A – to lead	141	6	Teutonic. Prosperous and joyful.
Adabelle First vowel A – to lead	14125335	24/6	Combination Ada and Belle. Joyous and beautiful.
Ambrosine First vowel A – to lead	142961955	42/6	Greek. Divine immortal one.
Antoinette First vowel A – to lead	1526955225	42/6	Latin. Beyond price. Fem. of Anthony.
Ava First vowel A – to lead	141	6	Latin. A bird.
Betina First vowel E – to communicate	252951	24/6	Hebrew. From Elizabeth, 'consecrated to God'.
Bryna First vowel A – to lead	29751	24/6	Irish. Strength with virtue.
Camilla First vowel A – to lead	3149331	24/6	Latin. Noble and righteous.
Celeste First vowel E – to communicate	3535125	24/6	Latin. Heavenly, a woman of beauty.
Christine First vowel I – intuition	389912955	51/6	French. A Christian.
Claudia First vowel A – to lead	3313491	24/6	Latin. The lame one.
Corinne First vowel O – to study	3699555	42/6	Greek. The maiden.
Cosette First vowel O – to study	3615225	24/6	French. Victorious army.
Davina First vowel A – to lead	414951	24/6	Hebrew. Beloved.
Dawn First vowel A – to lead	4155	15/6	Anglo-Saxon. Break of day.
Delta First vowel E – to communicate	54321	15/6	Greek. Fourth born.

Name	Number		Origin and meaning
Dara First vowel A – to lead	4191	15/6	Hebrew. Charity and compassion.
Daria First vowel A – to lead	41991	24/6	Greek. Wealthy queen.
Desma First vowel E – to communicate	45141	15/6	Greek. A pledge.
Diane First vowel I – intuition	49155	24/6	Latin. Goddess of the Moon.
Dilys First vowel I – intuition	49371	24/6	Welsh. Certain, perfect, genuine.
Dorcas First vowel O – to study	469311	24/6	Greek. Grace of the gazelle.
Dore First vowel O – to study	4695	24/6	French. Golden maiden.
Dorothy First vowel O – to study	4696287	42/6	Greek. Gift of God.
Edina First vowel E – to communicate	54951	24/6	Scottish form of Edwina.
Edna First vowel E – to communicate	5451	15/6	Hebrew. Rejuvenation, eternal youth.
Esme First vowel E – to communicate	5145	15/6	French. Beloved.
Estelle First vowel E – to communicate	5125335	24/6	French. Bright star.
Evadne First vowel E – to communicate	541455	24/6	Greek. Unknown meaning.
Flavia First vowel A – to lead	631491	24/6	Latin. Yellow haired.
Florence First vowel O – to study	63695535	42/6	Latin. A flower, or the city of Florence.
Frederica First vowel E – to communicate	695459931	51/6	Teutonic. Peaceful ruler.
Gay First vowel A – to lead	717	15/6	French. Lively.
Ginger First vowel I – intuition	795759	42/6	Latin (Virginia). Maidenly and pure.
Greta First vowel E – to communicate	79521	24/6	Teutonic version of Margaret, 'a pearl'.

Name	Number	Total	Origins and Meanings
Hermione	85949655	51/6	Greek. Of the earth.
First vowel E – to communicate			
Ileana	935151	24/6	Greek. Of Ilion (Troy).
First vowel I – intuition			
Ilona	93651	24/6	Greek (Helen). Light.
First vowel I – intuition			
Jacinda	1139541	24/6	Greek. Beautiful and comely.
First vowel A – to lead			
Janice	115935	24/6	Hebrew. God's gift of grace.
First vowel A – to lead			
Jemima	154941	24/6	Hebrew. The dove.
First vowel E – to communicate			
Joakima	1612941	24/6	Hebrew. Judgment of the Lord.
First vowel O – to study			
Jolie	16395	24/6	French. Pretty.
First vowel O – to study			
Juno	1356	15/6	Latin. Wife of Jupiter.
First vowel U – to protect			
Katharine	212819955	42/6	Greek. Pure maiden.
First vowel A – to lead			
Kim	294	15/6	Origin unknown. Noble chief.
First vowel I – intuition			
Kyna	2751	15/6	Gaelic. Great wisdom.
First vowel A – to lead			
Lemuela	3543531	24/6	Hebrew. Dedicated to God.
First vowel E – to communicate			
Lesley	351357	24/6	Celtic. Keeper of the grey fort.
First vowel E – to communicate			
Lili	3939	24/6	Latin. A lily.
First vowel I – intuition			
Lona	3651	15/6	Anglo-Spanish. Solitary watcher.
First vowel O – to study			
Lorna	36951	24/6	Latin (Laura). Laurel wreath.
First vowel O – to study			
Lotus	36231	15/6	Greek. Waterlily flower.
First vowel O – to study			

Louella 3635331 24/6 Anglo-Saxon. The
First vowel O – to study appeaser.

Lydia 37491 24/6 Greek. Cultured one.
First vowel I – intuition

Mabel 41253 15/6 Latin. Amiable and
First vowel A – to lead loving.

Maria 41991 24/6 Hebrew. Bitterness.
First vowel A – to lead

Marsha 419181 24/6 Latin. Belonging to
First vowel A – to lead Mars.

Matilda 4129341 24/6 Teutonic. Brave little
First vowel A – to lead maid.

Melba 45321 15/6 Greek. Soft and tender.
First vowel E – to communicate

Melissa 4539111 24/6 Greek. Honey bee.
First vowel E – to communicate

Merna 45951 24/6 Gaelic. Beloved.
First vowel E – to communicate

Micheline 493853955 51/6 Hebrew. Likeness to
First vowel I – intuition God. Fem. of Michael.

Netta 55221 15/6 Teutonic (Henrietta).
First vowel E – to communicate Ruler of home and
estate.

Noele 56535 24/6 Latin. Born at
First vowel O – to study Christmas time.

Nola 5631 15/6 Gaelic. Famous one.
First vowel O – to study

Nyssa 57111 15/6 Greek. Starting point.
First vowel A – to lead

Odette 645225 24/6 French. Home lover.
First vowel O – to study

Olwen 63555 24/6 Welsh. White track.
First vowel O – to study

Paula 71331 15/6 Latin. Small (fem. of
First vowel A – to lead Paul).

Peta 7521 15/6 Greek. Fem. of Peter,
First vowel E – to communicate 'the rock'.

Name	Number	Total	Origins and Meanings
Petra First vowel E – to communicate	75291	24/6	Greek. Fem. of Peter, 'the rock'.
Philippa First vowel I – intuition	78939771	51/6	Greek. Lover of horses.
Rae First vowel A – to lead	915	15/6	Middle English. A doe.
Rene First vowel E – to communicate	9555	24/6	Latin. Born again.
Rochelle First vowel O – to study	96385335	42/6	French. From the small rock.
Rosemary First vowel O – to study	96154197	42/6	Latin. Dew of the sea.
Ruella First vowel U – to protect	935331	24/6	Combination of Ruth and Ella.
Sally First vowel A – to lead	11337	15/6	Hebrew (Sarah). Princess.
Selina First vowel E – to communicate	153951	24/6	Greek. The Moon.
Shirley First vowel I – intuition	1899357	42/6	Anglo-Saxon. From the white meadow.
Stella First vowel E – to communicate	125331	15/6	French. Bright star.
Topaz First vowel O – to study	26718	24/6	Latin. The topaz gem.
Verna First vowel E – to communicate	45951	24/6	Latin. Spring-like.
Veronica First vowel E – to communicate	45965931	42/6	Latin. True image.
Wilfreda First vowel I – intuition	59369541	42/6	Teutonic. The peacemaker.
Zilla First vowel I – intuition	89331	24/6	Hebrew. Shadow.

Note: Refer to the section on Master Numbers 33 for Girls (pp. 153–5) for a further selection of Six names.

NUMBER SIX NAMES – BOYS

Name	Number	Total	Origins and Meanings
Abbott First vowel A – to lead	122622	15/6	Anglo-Saxon. Father of the abbey.
Adair First vowel A – to lead	14199	24/6	Gaelic. From the oak by the ford.
Alex First vowel A – to lead	1356	15/6	Greek. Helper and protector of mankind.
Alick First vowel A – to lead	13932	18/6	Greek. Helper and protector of mankind.
Ansel First vowel A – to lead	15153	15/6	French. Nobleman's follower.
Anyon First vowel A – to lead	15765	24/6	Celtic. Anvil. Fine forged characteristics.
Arden First vowel A – to lead	19455	24/6	Latin. Fiery, ardent loyal nature.
Arnett First vowel A – to lead	195522	24/6	French. Little eagle.
Asher First vowel A – to lead	11859	24/6	Hebrew. Laughing one, a happy lad.
Axel First vowel A – to lead	1653	15/6	Teutonic. Father of peace.
Bartholomew First vowel A – to lead	21928636455	51/6	Hebrew. Son of the furrows, one of the Apostles.
Bayard First vowel A – to lead	217194	24/6	Anglo-Saxon. Redhaired and strong.
Belden First vowel E – to communicate	253455	24/6	Anglo-Saxon. Dweller in the beautiful glen.
Benson First vowel E – to communicate	255165	24/6	Hebrew. Benjamin's son.
Blade First vowel A – to lead	23145	15/6	Anglo-Saxon. Prosperity and glory.
Blair First vowel A – to lead	23199	24/6	Gaelic. A place, or from the plain.

Name	Number	Total	Origins and Meanings
Boone First vowel O – to study	26655	24/6	Norse. The good one.
Borg First vowel O – to study	2697	24/6	Norse. Lives in a castle.
Bryan First vowel A – to lead	29715	24/6	Celtic. Powerful strength with virtue and honour.
Burne First vowel U – to protect	23955	24/6	Anglo-Saxon. A brook.
Clive First vowel I – intuition	33945	24/6	Anglo-Saxon. A cliff.
Corcoran First vowel O – to study	36936915	42/6	Gaelic. Reddish complexion.
Coyle First vowel O – to study	36735	24/6	Gaelic. Battle follower.
Daly First vowel A – to lead	4137	15/6	Gaelic. A counsellor.
Damian First vowel A – to lead	414915	24/6	Greek. Tamed one.
Dane First vowel A – to lead	4155	15/6	Anglo-Saxon. Man from Denmark.
Daryl First vowel A – to lead	41973	24/6	French. Beloved one.
Dean First vowel E – to communicate	4515	15/6	Anglo-Saxon. From the valley.
Demetrius First vowel E – to communicate	454529931	42/6	Greek. Belonging to Demeter.
Denis First vowel E – to communicate	45591	24/6	Greek. From Dionysus, god of wine.
Denman First vowel E – to communicate	455415	24/6	Anglo-Saxon. Resident in the valley.
Dion First vowel I – intuition	4965	24/6	Greek. From Dionysus, god of wine.
Dirk First vowel I – intuition	4992	24/6	Teutonic (Derek). Ruler of the people.
Dougal First vowel O – to study	463713	24/6	Celtic. From the dark stream.

Dow	465	15/6	Gaelic. Black haired.
First vowel O – to study			
Druce	49335	24/6	Celtic. Son of Drew.
First vowel U – to protect			
Durant	439152	24/6	Latin. Enduring friendship.
First vowel U – to protect			
Edan	5415	15/6	Celtic. Flame.
First vowel E – to communicate			
Ely	537	15/6	Hebrew (Eli). The Highest.
First vowel E – to communicate			
Emlyn	54375	24/6	Welsh form of Emil, 'industrious'.
First vowel E – to communicate			
Erasmus	5911431	24/6	Greek. Worthy of being loved.
First vowel E – to communicate			
Evan	5415	15/6	Gaelic. Well born young warrior.
First vowel E – to communicate			
Fabian	612915	24/6	Latin. Prosperous farmer.
First vowel A – to lead			
Gary	7197	24/6	Anglo-Saxon. Spearman.
First vowel A – to lead			
Gavyn	71475	24/6	Celtic. The battle hawk.
First vowel A – to lead			
Geoffrey	75666957	51/6	Teutonic. God's divine peace.
First vowel E – to communicate			
Grant	79152	24/6	French. The great one.
First vowel A – to lead			
Gwyn	7575	24/6	Celtic. The blond one.
No vowel, I sound			
Haley	81357	24/6	Gaelic. The ingenious one.
First vowel A – to lead			
Hugo	8376	24/6	Teutonic. Brilliant, shining mind.
First vowel U – to protect			
Humphrey	83478957	51/6	Teutonic. Protector of the peace.
First vowel U – to protect			
Iain	9195	24/6	Celtic form of John, 'God's gracious gift'.
First vowel I – intuition			
Ian	915	15/6	Celtic form of John, 'God's gracious gift'.
First vowel I – intuition			

Name	Number	Total	Origins and Meanings
Isaac First vowel I – intuition	91113	15/6	Hebrew. The laughing one.
Jasper First vowel A – to lead	111759	24/6	Persian. Master of the treasure.
Jeremiah First vowel E – to communicate	15954918	42/6	Hebrew. Exalted by the Lord.
Joel First vowel O – to study	1653	15/6	Hebrew. 'The Lord is God'.
Karl First vowel A – to lead	2193	15/6	Teutonic (Charles). The strong man.
Lachlan First vowel A – to lead	3138315	24/6	Celtic. Warlike.
Linford First vowel I – intuition	3956694	42/6	Anglo-Saxon. From the lime tree ford.
Lucian First vowel U – to protect	333915	24/6	Latin. Light.
Lyn No vowel, I sound	375	15/6	Welsh. From the pool or waterfall.
Malcolm First vowel A – to lead	4133634	24/6	Celtic. The dove or follower of St. Columbus.
Maximilian First vowel A – to lead	4169493915	51/6	Latin. The greatest, most excellent.
Meredydd First vowel E – to communicate	45954744	42/6	Welsh. Guardian from the sea.
Merrill First vowel E – to communicate	4599933	42/6	French. Little famous one.
Proctor First vowel O – to study	7963269	42/6	Latin. The administrator.
Rae First vowel A – to lead	915	15/6	French. The sovereign. Or diminutive of Raymond.
René First vowel E – to communicate	9555	24/6	Teutonic (Reginald). Mighty and powerful.
Rolf First vowel O – to study	9636	24/6	Teutonic. Famous wolf.

Ruben   93255   24/6   Hebrew. 'Behold a son'.
First vowel U – to protect

Seamus   151431   15/6   Irish (James). The
First vowel E – to communicate   supplanter.

Seumas   153411   15/6   Gaelic (James). The
First vowel E – to communicate   supplanter.

Shaw   1815   15/6   Anglo-Saxon. From the
First vowel A – to lead   grove.

Stanley   1215357   24/6   Anglo-Saxon. From the
First vowel A – to lead   stony meadow.

Terrence   25995535   43/7   Latin. Smooth,
First vowel E – to communicate   polished and tender.

Troy   2967   24/6   French. From the land
First vowel O – to study   of the people with curly
    hair.

Truman   293415   24/6   Anglo-Saxon. Faithful
First vowel U – to protect   follower.

Urson   39165   24/6   Latin. Little bear.
First vowel U – to protect

Wade   5145   15/6   Anglo-Saxon. Mover,
First vowel A – to lead   wanderer.

York   7692   24/6   Latin/Anglo-Saxon/Celtic.
First vowel O – to study   Sacred tree/Boar's
    estate/Yew tree estate.

Zedekiah   85452918   42/6   Hebrew. The Lord's
First vowel E – to communicate   justice.

Note: Refer to the section on Master Numbers 33 for Boys
(pp. 156–60) for a further selection of Six names.

NUMBER SEVEN QUALITIES

If your birth number reduces to one of the Seven vibrations, you are imaginative and creative, with musical or poetic ability. You may be artistic enough to paint or sketch, or feel the need to design your own clothes. Seven is quite a spiritual number and quite charitable. It is, however, prone to dream and plan rather than to do, as the number also requires reassurance and sometimes support to feel safe and secure enough to begin its projects.

Seven is the number of the planet Neptune and sharpens the intuitive senses and the imagination of people born under it. Care must, however, be taken that you separate imaginary fears and phobias from the realities of your life. Sevens find it harder to trust others. However, once their approval is won they would give you the shirt off their backs.

Sevens should go for the jobs which they feel assured are worthwhile, and any caring, humanitarian career, such as nursing or in the social services can satisfy this need. Most Sevens need a push start to get going. However, once rolling, they see projects through to the end and expect the same from their associates.

If you are a Seven your best matches are with other Sevens, Fives or Twos.

Any number of this vibration will strengthen the birth number and your child's personality. Or choose one of the three directional numbers (pp. 7–8).

TYPES OF SEVENS

16/7 This is an independent Seven with a need to brighten up the environment in which he or she lives. Theirs is a combination of artistic flair and the drive to accomplish, though with a slight tendency to be a little ahead of their time. This number needs to separate the feeling it sometimes has of not belonging and should mix more with other types.

25/7 Imagination, compassion and communication ability are qualities to be admired in this type of Seven. Languages and a literary career are emphasised, and long term partnerships. This Seven can work all hours of the day as long as he feels his efforts will be noticed by those for whom he works.

34/7 These are the creative designers of society, the ones who invent and create our futures in order that others may put them to good use. They are the cogs of a watch, rarely seen in public, but without them society as we know it would stagnate, and progress would come to a halt.

43/7 A reverse of the above in so much as this type of Seven displays creativity more at home than at work. The ideas and imagination are directed towards making the family home safer and easier to live in. Decor in the home may be unusual.

52/7 This type of Seven communicates to the masses. Fictional authors, actors or playwrights could do a lot worse than to have this as a birth or name number. It gives the ability to communicate the imagination to the general public. Although extrovert outwardly, this is a very private, inner number and must have a safe and secluded retreat to retire to for recuperation.

61/7 Not known to us as a name number.

NUMBER SEVEN NAMES – GIRLS

Name	Number	Total	Origins and Meanings
Adrienne First vowel A – to lead	14995555	43/7	Latin. Dark lady from the sea.
Alethea First vowel A – to lead	1352851	25/7	Greek. Truth.
Alison First vowel A – to lead	139165	25/7	Combination of Alice and Louise, 'truthful warrior maid'.
Alta First vowel A – to lead	1321	7	Latin. Tall in spirit.
Amanda First vowel A – to lead	141541	16/7	Latin. Worthy of being loved.
Ana First vowel A – to lead	151	7	Hebrew. Full of grace.
Andrea First vowel A – to lead	154951	25/7	Latin. Womanly, feminine charm.
Angelica First vowel A – to lead	15753931	34/7	Latin. Angelic one.
Anne First vowel A – to lead	1555	16/7	Hebrew. Full of grace.
Annette First vowel A – to lead	1555225	25/7	Hebrew. Full of grace.
Arabella First vowel A – to lead	19125331	25/7	Latin. Beautiful altar.
Ariadne First vowel A – to lead	1991455	34/7	Greek. Holy one.
Athalia First vowel A – to lead	1281391	25/7	Hebrew. 'God is exalted'.
Avena First vowel A – to lead	14551	16/7	Latin. Oatfield, rich golden hair.
Baptista First vowel A – to lead	21729121	25/7	Latin. Baptised, free from sin.

Barbara 2192191 25/7 Latin. Beautiful
First vowel A – to lead stranger.

Beatrix 2512996 34/7 Latin. She who brings
First vowel E – to communicate joy.

Benigna 2559751 34/7 Latin. Gentle and kind,
First vowel E – to communicate a great lady.

Berenice 25955935 43/7 Greek. Herald of
First vowel E – to communicate victory.

Bette 25225 16/7 Hebrew. Derived from
First vowel E – to communicate Elizabeth, 'consecrated
to God'.

Bliss 23911 16/7 Old English. Gladness
First vowel I – intuition and joy.

Bonita 265921 25/7 Latin. Sweet and good.
First vowel O – to study

Carmel 319453 25/7 Hebrew. God's fruitful
First vowel A – to lead vineyard.

Carissa 3199111 25/7 Latin. Most dear.
First vowel A – to lead

Carita 319921 25/7 Latin. Beloved little
First vowel A – to lead one.

Carolyn 3196375 34/7 Teutonic. Little woman,
First vowel A – to lead born to command.

Chiquita 38983921 43/7 Spanish. Little one.
First vowel I – intuition

Chloe 38365 25/7 Greek. Fresh, young
First vowel O – to study blossom.

Christabel 3899121253 43/7 Latin. Beautiful,
First vowel I – intuition bright-faced Christian.

Cleva 33541 16/7 Old English. Cliff
First vowel E – to communicate dweller.

Cosina 361951 25/7 Greek. World harmony.
First vowel O – to study

Delcine 4533955 34/7 Latin. Sweet and
First vowel E – to communicate charming.

Devona 454651 25/7 English. From Devon.
First vowel E – to communicate

Name	Number	Total	Origins and Meanings
Dolores First vowel O – to study	4636951	34/7	Spanish. Lady of sorrow.
Doreen First vowel O – to study	469555	34/7	Gaelic. Golden girl.
Edana First vowel E – to communicate	54151	16/7	Gaelic. Little fiery one.
Eirlys First vowel E – to communicate	599371	34/7	Welsh. Snowdrop.
Eleanor First vowel E – to communicate	5351569	34/7	French. Mediaeval form of Helen.
Elga First vowel E – to communicate	5371	16/7	Slavonic. Consecrated.
Elizabeth First vowel E – to communicate	539812528	43/7	Hebrew. Consecrated to God.
Ethyl First vowel E – to communicate	52873	25/7	Teutonic. Noble maiden.
Eulalia First vowel E – to communicate	5331391	25/7	Greek. Fair spoken one.
Fern First vowel E – to communicate	6595	25/7	Anglo-Saxon. Fernlike.
Flora First vowel O – to study	63691	25/7	Latin. A flower.
Flower First vowel O – to study	636559	34/7	English. English version of Flora.
Francesca First vowel A – to lead	691535131	34/7	Latin. Free.
Franchon First vowel A – to lead	69153865	43/7	French. Free being.
Francine First vowel A – to lead	69153955	43/7	Latin. Free.
Freda First vowel E – to communicate	69541	25/7	Teutonic. Peace, one who is calm.
Gael First vowel A – to lead	7153	16/7	Celtic, the lively one, or Hebrew (Abigail), 'Father rejoiced'.
Gale First vowel A – to lead	7135	16/7	Celtic, the lively one, or Hebrew (Abigail), 'Father rejoiced'.

Gitana	792151	25/7	Spanish. Gypsy.
First vowel I – intuition			
Grace	79135	25/7	Latin. The graceful one.
First vowel A – to lead			
Gracie	791395	34/7	Latin. The graceful one.
First vowel A – to lead			
Guinevere	739554595	52/7	Celtic. White phantom.
First vowel U – to protect			
Harriet	8199952	43/7	Teutonic. Ruler of home and estate.
First vowel A – to lead			
Hazel	81853	25/7	English. The hazel tree.
First vowel A – to lead			
Hilda	89341	25/7	Teutonic. Battle maid.
First vowel I – intuition			
Honor	86569	34/7	Latin. Honour.
First vowel O – to study			
Huette	835225	25/7	Anglo-Saxon. Brilliant thinker.
First vowel U – to protect			
Ignatia	9751291	34/7	Latin. Fiery ardour.
First vowel I – intuition			
Ingrid	957994	43/7	Norse. Hero's daughter.
First vowel I – intuition			
Ione	9655	25/7	Greek. Violet coloured stone.
First vowel I – intuition			
Jacqueline	1138353955	43/7	Hebrew. The supplanter.
First vowel A – to lead			
Jan	115	7	Hebrew. God's gift of grace.
First vowel A – to lead			
Jill	1933	16/7	Latin. Youthful.
First vowel I – intuition			
Kathryn	2128975	34/7	Greek. Pure maiden.
First vowel A – to lead			
Larissa	3199111	25/7	Greek. Cheerful maiden.
First vowel A – to lead			
Lilith	393928	34/7	Arabic. Woman of the night.
First vowel I – intuition			
Lindsey	3954157	34/7	Anglo-Saxon. Pool island.
First vowel I – intuition			

Name	Number	Total	Origins and Meanings
Lucianne First vowel U – to protect	33391555	34/7	Combination of Lucy and Anne.
Lucilla First vowel U – to protect	3339331	25/7	Latin. Light.
Lucy First vowel U – to protect	3337	16/7	Latin. Light.
Lynne First vowel E – to communicate	37555	25/7	Celtic. A waterfall.
Lynnette First vowel E – to communicate	37555225	34/7	French. Sweet bird.
Lysette First vowel E – to communicate	3715225	25/7	Hebrew. Derived from Elizabeth, 'consecrated to God'.
Margarita First vowel A – to lead	419719921	43/7	Latin. A pearl.
Marigold First vowel A – to lead	41997634	43/7	English. Golden flower girl.
Marion First vowel A – to lead	419965	34/7	Hebrew. Bitter and graceful.
Martha First vowel A – to lead	419281	25/7	Arabic. Mistress.
Michaela First vowel I – intuition	49381531	34/7	Hebrew. Likeness to God.
Millicent First vowel I – intuition	493393552	43/7	Teutonic. Strong and industrious.
Mona First vowel O – to study	4651	16/7	Latin. Derived from Monica, 'advice giver'.
Nanette First vowel A – to lead	5155225	25/7	Hebrew (Anne). Full of grace.
Naomi First vowel A – to lead	51649	25/7	Hebrew. The pleasant one.
Nara First vowel A – to lead	5191	16/7	Latin. Born at Christmas time.
Nathalie First vowel A – to lead	51281395	34/7	Latin. Born at Christmas time.
Nixie First vowel I – intuition	59695	34/7	Teutonic. Water sprite.

Norma   56941   25/7   Latin. A pattern or rule.
First vowel O – to study

Novia   56491   25/7   Latin. Newcomer.
First vowel O – to study

Pearl   75193   25/7   Latin. Precious jewel.
First vowel E – to communicate

Poppy   76777   34/7   Latin. Red flower.
First vowel O – to study

Portia   769291   34/7   Latin. Offering to God.
First vowel O – to study

Penelope   75553675   43/7   Greek. The weaver.
First vowel E – to communicate

Rana   9151   16/7   Sanskrit. Of royal birth.
First vowel A – to lead

Roberta   9625921   34/7   Anglo-Saxon. Of
First vowel O – to study   shining fame.

Rosalie   9611395   34/7   Greek. The rose.
First vowel O – to study

Rula   9331   16/7   Latin. A sovereign,
First vowel U – to protect   ruler by right.

Sheena   185551   25/7   Gaelic form of Jane,
First vowel E – to communicate   'God's gift of grace'.

Sian   1915   16/7   Celtic version of Jane,
First vowel I – intuition   'God's gift of grace'.

Stephanie   125781595   43/7   Greek. A crown,
First vowel E – to communicate   garland.

Susannah   13115518   25/7   Hebrew. Graceful lily.
First vowel U – to protect

Sylvia   173491   25/7   Latin. From the forest.
First vowel I – intuition

Tabitha   2129281   25/7   Aramaic. One of gentle
First vowel A – to lead   grace, gazelle.

Tansy   21517   16/7   Latin. Tenacious,
First vowel A – to lead   determined woman.

Tanya   21571   16/7   Greek and Russian.
First vowel A – to lead   Queen of the fairies.

Theola   285631   25/7   Greek. Sent from God.
First vowel E – to communicate

Name	Number	Total	Origins and Meanings
Thera First vowel E – to communicate	28591	25/7	Greek. Wild, untamed one.
Trudy First vowel U – to protect	29347	25/7	Teutonic. Loved one.
Ula First vowel U – to protect	331	7	Celtic. Jewel of the sea.
Victoria First vowel I – intuition	49326991	43/7	Latin. The victorious one.
Vita First vowel I – intuition	4921	16/7	Latin. Life, one who likes living.
Wanda First vowel A – to lead	51541	16/7	Teutonic. Wanderer.
Wilhelmina First vowel I – intuition	5938534951	52/7	Teutonic. Protectress.
Winifred First vowel I – intuition	59596954	52/7	Teutonic. Peaceful friend.
Ynez First vowel E – to communicate	7558	25/7	Greek (Agnes). Pure and chaste.
Yvette First vowel E – to communicate	745225	25/7	French. Archer with the yew bow.

NUMBER SEVEN NAMES – BOYS

Name	Number	Total	Origins and Meanings
Adon First vowel A – to lead	1465	16/7	Hebrew. Lord. Sacred Hebrew word for God.
Albern First vowel A – to lead	132595	25/7	Anglo-Saxon. Noble warrior.
Alexis First vowel A – to lead	135691	25/7	Greek (Alexander). Helper and protector of mankind.
Altman First vowel A – to lead	132415	16/7	Teutonic. Wise old man.
Alyn First vowel A – to lead	1375	16/7	Gaelic. Cheerful harmony.
Aneirin First vowel A – to lead	1559995	43/7	Celtic. Truly goldern.
Anthony First vowel A – to lead	1528657	34/7	Latin. A man without peer.
Ashley First vowel A – to lead	118357	25/7	Anglo-Saxon. Dweller in the ash tree meadow.
Barton First vowel A – to lead	219265	25/7	Anglo-Saxon. Barley farmer.
Basil First vowel A – to lead	21193	16/7	Greek. Kingly.
Benton First vowel E – to communicate	255265	25/7	Anglo-Saxon. From the town on the moors.
Blaine First vowel A – to lead	231955	25/7	Greek. Thin and hungry-looking.
Boot First vowel O – to study	2662	16/7	Teutonic. Herald.
Botolf First vowel O – to study	262636	25/7	Anglo-Saxon. Herald wolf.
Boyne First vowel O – to study	26755	25/7	Gaelic. White cow. A rare person.
Brad First vowel A – to lead	2914	16/7	Anglo-Saxon. Broad.

Name	Number	Total	Origins and Meanings
Bruno First vowel U – to protect	29356	25/7	Teutonic. Brown haired man.
Burt First vowel U – to protect	2392	16/7	Anglo-Saxon. Of bright glorious fame.
Calvin First vowel A – to lead	313495	25/7	Latin. Bald.
Carey First vowel A – to lead	31957	25/7	Celtic. One who lives in a castle.
Carl First vowel A – to lead	3193	16/7	Teutonic. The strong man.
Carroll First vowel A – to lead	3199633	34/7	Gaelic. The champion.
Chad First vowel A – to lead	3814	16/7	Anglo-Saxon. Warlike.
Chance First vowel A – to lead	381535	25/7	Anglo-Saxon. Good fortune.
Chesney First vowel E – to communicate	3851557	34/7	French. Oak forest dweller.
Clarence First vowel A – to lead	33195535	34/7	Latin/Anglo-Saxon. Famous, illustrious.
Colm First vowel O – to study	3634	16/7	Latin. Dove.
Connor First vowel O – to study	365569	34/7	Gaelic. High desire.
Constant First vowel O – to study	36512152	25/7	Latin. Firm, unwavering.
Crispin First vowel I – intuition	3991795	43/7	Latin. Curly haired.
Darrell First vowel A – to lead	4199533	34/7	French. Beloved one.
Denzil First vowel E – to communicate	455893	34/7	Greek. From Dionysus, the god of wine.
Derek First vowel E – to communicate	45952	25/7	Teutonic. Ruler of the people.
Derry First vowel E – to communicate	45997	34/7	Gaelic. The red one.

Doran   46915   25/7   Celtic. The stranger.
First vowel O – to study

Dorian   469915   34/7   Greek. Man from Doria.
First vowel O – to study

Douglas   4637311   25/7   Celtic. From the dark
First vowel O – to study   stream.

Doyle   46735   25/7   Gaelic. Dark haired
First vowel O – to study   stranger.

Edmund   544354   25/7   Anglo-Saxon. Rich
First vowel E – to communicate   guardian.

Ellard   533194   25/7   Anglo-Saxon. Noble,
First vowel E – to communicate   brave.

Engelbert   557532592   43/7   Teutonic. Bright angel.
First vowel E – to communicate

Ennis   55591   25/7   Gaelic. The only choice.
First vowel E – to communicate

Ephraim   5789194   43/7   Hebrew. Abounding in
First vowel E – to communicate   fruitfulness.

Esmond   514654   25/7   Anglo-Saxon. Gracious
First vowel E – to communicate   protector.

Ewan   5515   16/7   Gaelic. Well born young
First vowel E – to communicate   warrior.

Filip   69397   34/7   Greek. Lover of horses.
First vowel I – intuition

Finn   6955   25/7   Gaelic. Fairhaired.
First vowel I – intuition

Fitz   6928   25/7   Anglo-French. Son.
First vowel I – intuition

Flint   63952   25/7   Anglo-Saxon. The
First vowel I – intuition   stream.

Francis   6915391   34/7   Latin. Free man.
First vowel A – to lead

Frederick   695459932   52/7   Teutonic. Peaceful
First vowel E – to communicate   ruler.

Georg   75697   34/7   Greek. The farmer.
First vowel E – to communicate

Giles   79351   25/7   Latin. Shield bearer.
First vowel I – intuition

Name	Number	Total	Origins and Meanings
Girvin First vowel I – intuition	799495	43/7	Gaelic. Little rough one.
Glenn First vowel E – to communicate	73555	25/7	Celtic. From the valley.
Hank First vowel A – to lead	8152	16/7	Teutonic. Ruler of the estate.
Haig First vowel A – to lead	8197	25/7	Anglo-Saxon. One who lives in an enclosure.
Harry First vowel A – to lead	81997	34/7	Anglo-Saxon. Army commander.
Harvey First vowel A – to lead	819457	34/7	Teutonic. Army warrior.
Henry First vowel E – to communicate	85597	34/7	Teutonic. Ruler of the estate.
Huw First vowel U – to protect	835	16/7	Teutonic. Brilliant, thinker.
Hyman First vowel A – to lead	87415	25/7	Hebrew. Life, the divine spark.
Immanuel First vowel I – intuition	94415353	34/7	Hebrew. 'God is with us'.
Isidore First vowel I – intuition	9194695	43/7	Greek. The gift of Isis.
Jack First vowel A – to lead	1132	7	Hebrew. God's gracious gift.
Keegan First vowel E – to communicate	255715	25/7	Celtic. Little fiery one.
Kevin First vowel E – to communicate	25495	25/7	Gaelic. Kind, gentle and lovable.
Kurt First vowel U – to protect	2392	16/7	Teutonic. Brave commander.
Laurence First vowel A – to lead	31395535	34/7	Latin. Crowned with laurels.
Leopold First vowel E – to communicate	3567634	34/7	Teutonic. Brave for the people.
Lester First vowel E – to communicate	351259	25/7	Anglo-Saxon. From the army camp.

Lincoln	3953635	34/7	Celtic. From the place by the pool.
First vowel I – intuition			
Lindsey	3954157	34/7	Anglo-Saxon. Pool island.
First vowel I – intuition			
Luis	3391	16/7	Teutonic. Famous warrior.
First vowel U – to protect			
Maddox	414466	25/7	Welsh. Beneficient.
First vowel A – to lead			
Manfred	4156954	34/7	Anglo-Saxon. Peaceful hero.
First vowel A – to lead			
Marcel	419353	25/7	Latin. Little flower of Mars.
First vowel A – to lead			
Marion	419965	34/7	French. Bitter.
First vowel A – to lead			
Mark	4192	16/7	Latin. Follower of Mars.
First vowel A – to lead			
Maurice	4139935	34/7	Latin. Moorish looking, dark complexion.
First vowel A – to lead			
Mervyn	459475	34/7	Anglo-Saxon (Marvin). Famous friend.
First vowel E – to communicate			
Micah	49318	25/7	Hebrew (Michael). Like unto the Lord.
First vowel I – intuition			
Morse	46915	25/7	Anglo-Saxon. Maurice's son.
First vowel O – to study			
Nelson	553165	25/7	Celtic. Son of Neal.
First vowel E – to communicate			
Neville	5549335	34/7	Latin. From the new town.
First vowel E – to communicate			
Ninian	595915	34/7	An early British saint's name.
First vowel I – intuition			
Orlando	6931546	34/7	Teutonic. From the famed land.
First vowel O – to study			
Otto	6226	16/7	Teutonic. Wealthy, prosperous man.
First vowel O – to study			
Padraic	7149193	34/7	Latin (Patrick). One of noble birth.
First vowel A – to lead			
Pascal	711313	16/7	Italian. Easter born.
First vowel A – to lead			

Name	Number	Total	Origins and Meanings
Philip First vowel I – intuition	789397	43/7	Greek. Lover of horses.
Quinlan First vowel U – to protect	8395315	34/7	Gaelic. The well formed one.
Rafael First vowel A – to lead	916153	25/7	Hebrew. Healed by God.
Ramon First vowel A – to lead	91465	25/7	Teutonic. Wise protection.
Randolf First vowel A – to lead	9154636	34/7	Old English. Shield wolf.
Randolph First vowel A – to lead	91546378	43/7	Old English. Shield wolf.
Raphael First vowel A – to lead	9178153	34/7	Hebrew. Healed by God.
Reginald First vowel E – to communicate	95795134	43/7	Teutonic. Mighty and powerful ruler.
Remington First vowel E – to communicate	954957265	52/7	Anglo-Saxon. From the farm where blackbirds sing.
Rhys No vowel, I sound	9871	25/7	Celtic. The ardent one.
Richard First vowel I – intuition	9938194	43/7	Teutonic. Wealthy and powerful.
Rigby First vowel I – intuition	99727	34/7	Anglo-Saxon. Valley of the ruler.
Russell First vowel U – to protect	9311533	25/7	Anglo-Saxon. Red as a fox.
Ryder First vowel E – to communicate	97459	34/7	Anglo-Saxon. Horse-rider, knight.
Seth First vowel E – to communicate	1528	16/7	Hebrew. Appointed by God.
Sian First vowel I – intuition	1915	16/7	Hebrew (John). God's gracious gift.
Sloan First vowel O – to study	13615	16/7	Gaelic. Warrior.
Stewart First vowel E – to communicate	1255192	25/7	Anglo-Saxon. The steward.

Terence 2595535 34/7 Latin. Smooth,
First vowel E – to communicate polished and tender.

Thornton 28695265 43/7 Anglo-Saxon. From the
First vowel O – to study thorny place.

Todd 2644 16/7 Origin unknown. The
First vowel O – to study fox.

Tyrone 279655 34/7 Greek. The sovereign.
First vowel O – to study

Vernon 459565 34/7 Latin. Growing,
First vowel E – to communicate flourishing.

Walter 513259 25/7 Teutonic. Mighty
First vowel A – to lead warrior.

Warren 519955 34/7 Teutonic. The
First vowel A – to lead gamekeeper.

Willard 5933194 34/7 Anglo-Saxon. Resolute
First vowel I – intuition or brave.

William 5933914 34/7 Teutonic. Determined
First vowel I – intuition protector.

Wolfram 5636914 34/7 Teutonic. Respected
First vowel O – to study and feared.

Xavier 614959 34/7 Spanish, new house
First vowel A – to lead owner. Arabic, bright.

NUMBER EIGHT QUALITIES

If your birth number reduces to an Eight you have been blessed with the ability to build on the material plane. Consolidation, materialism, business acumen and work involving mines and the earth itself are in your favour.

Eight is a much misunderstood vibration. Its corresponding planet is Saturn, much feared and wrongly accused in the past. Eight as a number force is hard-working, industrious, patient and persevering, therefore, get-rich-quick schemes are not really for an Eight. An Eight's path may be long, hard and stony but he knows that at the end there is a pasture of riches that go beyond the material. A lot of wealth and power may be wielded by Eights, but it is this wealth that creates the jobs and prosperity of others.

Eights may prefer their own company and do not mix well if they feel their work is incomplete. A good career for an Eight who is not self-employed would be in politics, banking, stock markets or mining. Once an Eight has satisfied its need for security it can be one of the more charitable of number vibrations, though usually behind the scenes in some way.

Eights get on best with other Eights, Fours or Ones.

Any number of this vibration will strengthen the birth number and your child's personality. Or choose one of the three directional numbers (pp. 7–8).

TYPES OF EIGHTS

17/8 blends leadership with compassion and imagination. This type of Eight will never ask you to do what he would not do himself, and demonstrates by example. But don't cross this Eight; he can be very ruthless.

26/8 blends the material with the spiritual. This type of Eight is one of the few Eights who actively seek partnerships in business and at home. This Eight has artistic inclinations and may even be a poet under its harder outer shell.

35/8 blends philosophy and communication. This Eight can be Jack of all trades. There is the ability to plan, execute and conclude projects and ambitions and few obstacles would be able to hold this Eight back once he has set his aim.

44/8 The double 4 of this type of Eight can lead to a degree of uncertainty. There is not much rest for this type of Eight as he always has a nagging doubt that he should do a little more and is never really content with what he has. This Eight is a little too much of a perfectionist, both with himself and others.

53/8 blends communication and travel, though this type of Eight is more of a doer than a planner. He or she is probably the most active physically of all Eight types and yet also the one most likely to enjoy life to its full. This Eight is one of the last to settle down and yet the first to achieve security. A lucky eight.

62/8 Not known to us in forenames.

NUMBER EIGHT NAMES – GIRLS

Name	Number	Total	Origins and Meanings
Adorna First vowel A – to lead	146951	26/8	Latin. Adorned with jewels.
Alexandra First vowel A – to lead	135615491	35/8	Greek. Helper of mankind.
Alura First vowel A – to lead	13391	17/8	Anglo-Saxon. Divine counsellor.
Anabel First vowel A – to lead	151253	17/8	Latin. Sweet.
Annemarie First vowel A – to lead	155541995	44/8	Hebrew. Combination of Anne, 'full of grace', and Mary, 'bitterness'.
Astrid First vowel A – to lead	112994	26/8	Norse. Divine strength.
Athene First vowel A – to lead	128555	26/8	Greek. Goddess of wisdom.
Avril First vowel A – to lead	14993	26/8	Old English. Slayer of the boar.
Basilia First vowel A – to lead	2119391	26/8	Greek. Queenly, regal.
Bea First vowel E – to communicate	251	8	Latin. Derived from Beatrice, 'she who brings joy'.
Beryl First vowel E – to communicate	25973	26/8	Greek. Precious jewel.
Beverly First vowel E – to communicate	2545937	35/8	Anglo-Saxon. Ambitious one.
Brenda First vowel E – to communicate	295541	26/8	Teutonic, fiery, or Irish, raven.
Cadence First vowel A – to lead	3145535	26/8	Latin. Rhythmic, graceful and charming.

Carla 31931 17/8
First vowel A – to lead
Teutonic. A variation of Caroline, 'little woman, born to command'.

Cassandra 311115491 26/8
First vowel A – to lead
Greek. Phophetess ignored by men.

Casta 31121 8
First vowel A – to lead
Latin. Of pure upbringing.

Cheryl 385973 35/8
First vowel E – to communicate
French. Dear, beloved one.

Clara 33191 17/8
First vowel A – to lead
Latin. Bright shining girl.

Clarabelle 3319125335 35/8
First vowel A – to lead
Latin/French. Bright, shining beauty.

Cleo 3356 17/8
First vowel E – to communicate
Greek. Shortened form of Cleopatra, 'her father's glory'.

Colette 3635225 26/8
First vowel O – to study
Latin. Victorious.

Crystal 3971213 26/8
First vowel A – to lead
Greek. Ice, crystal.

Cynthia 3752891 35/8
First vowel I – intuition
Greek. Moon goddess.

Cyrilla 3799331 35/8
First vowel I – intuition
Latin. Lordly one.

Danielle 41595335 35/8
First vowel A – to lead
Hebrew. 'God is my judge'.

Deborah 4526918 35/8
First vowel E – to communicate
Hebrew. The bee, industrious.

Docila 463931 26/8
First vowel O – to study
Latin. Gentle teacher.

Eartha 519281 26/8
First vowel E – to communicate
Old English. Of the earth.

Eliza 53981 26/8
First vowel E – to communicate
Hebrew (Elizabeth). Consecrated to God.

Elsbeth 5312528 26/8
First vowel E – to communicate
Hebrew (Elizabeth). Consecrated to God.

Elysia 537191 26/8
First vowel E – to communicate
Greek. Blissful sweetness.

Name	Number	Total	Origins and Meanings
Erika First vowel E – to communicate	59921	26/8	Norse. Powerful ruler. Fem. of Eric.
Eugenia First vowel E – to communicate	5375591	35/8	Greek. Well born, of noble family.
Faith First vowel A – to lead	61928	26/8	Teutonic. Trust in God.
Felicity First vowel E – to communicate	65393927	44/8	Latin. Joyous one.
Fleur First vowel E – to communicate	63539	26/8	French. Flower.
Gabrielle First vowel A – to lead	712995335	44/8	Hebrew. Woman of God.
Gaynor First vowel A – to lead	717569	35/8	Gaelic. Daughter of the blond haired one.
Georgia First vowel E – to communicate	7569791	44/8	Greek. Fem. of George, 'the farmer'.
Gertrude First vowel E – to communicate	75929345	44/8	Teutonic. Spear maiden, Valkyrie.
Gisela First vowel I – intuition	791531	26/8	Teutonic. A promise.
Glenna First vowel E – to communicate	735551	26/8	Celtic. From the valley.
Glennis First vowel E – to communicate	7355591	35/8	Celtic. From the valley.
Gloria First vowel O – to study	736991	35/8	Latin. Glorious. An illustrious person.
Greer First vowel E – to communicate	79559	35/8	Greek. The watchful mother.
Helen First vowel E – to communicate	85355	26/8	Greek. Light.
Honora First vowel O – to study	865691	35/8	Latin. Honour.
Hope First vowel O – to study	8675	26/8	Anglo-Saxon. Cheerful optimism.
Jacquetta First vowel A – to lead	113835221	26/8	Hebrew. The supplanter.

Janis	11591	17/8	Hebrew. God's gift of grace.
First vowel A – to lead			
Jeanette	15155225	26/8	Hebrew. God's gift of grace.
First vowel E – to communicate			
Jocelyne	16353755	35/8	Latin. Fair and just. Fem. of Justin.
First vowel O – to study			
Judi	1349	17/8	Hebrew. Admired, praised.
First vowel U – to protect			
Julia	13391	17/8	Latin. Youthful.
First vowel U – to protect			
Justine	1312955	26/8	Latin (Jocelyn). Fair and just.
First vowel U – to protect			
Lala	3131	8	Slavonic. Tulip flower.
First vowel A – to lead			
Laura	31391	17/8	Latin. Laurel wreath, victor's crown.
First vowel A – to lead			
Lauren	313955	26/8	Latin. Laurel wreath.
First vowel A – to lead			
Leah	3518	17/8	Hebrew. The weary one.
First vowel E – to communicate			
Leonora	3565691	35/8	Greek (Helen). Light.
First vowel E – to communicate			
Liliane	3939155	35/8	Latin. A lily.
First vowel I – intuition			
Lilias	393911	26/8	Latin. A lily.
First vowel I – intuition			
Lucretia	33395291	35/8	Latin. A rich reward.
First vowel U – to protect			
Magdalene	417413555	35/8	Greek. Tower of strength.
First vowel A – to lead			
Marjorie	41916995	44/8	Latin. A pearl.
First vowel A – to lead			
Merle	45935	26/8	Latin. The blackbird.
First vowel E – to communicate			
Messina	4511951	26/8	Latin. The middle child.
First vowel E – to communicate			
Myrna	47951	26/8	Gaelic. Beloved.
First vowel A – to lead			

Name	Number	Total	Origins and Meanings
Natalie First vowel A – to lead	5121395	26/8	Latin. Born at Christmas time.
Nichola First vowel I – intuition	5938631	35/8	Greek. The people's victory.
Nikola First vowel I – intuition	592631	26/8	Greek. Leader of the people.
Noreen First vowel O – to study	569555	35/8	Latin. Derived from Honora, 'honour'.
Olga First vowel O – to study	6371	17/8	Teutonic. Holy, anointed to God.
Olwyn First vowel O – to study	63575	26/8	Welsh. White/track.
Opal First vowel O – to study	6713	17/8	Latin. Precious jewel.
Philantha First vowel I – intuition	789315281	44/8	Greek. Lover of flowers.
Polly First vowel O – to study	76337	26/8	Hebrew (Mary). Bitterness.
Ramona First vowel A – to lead	914651	26/8	Teutonic. Wise protector.
Raphaela First vowel A – to lead	91781531	35/8	Hebrew. Blessed healer.
Richenda First vowel I – intuition	99385541	44/8	Teutonic. Powerful ruler. Fem. of Richard.
Rosetta First vowel O – to study	9615221	26/8	Greek. The rose.
Samara First vowel A – to lead	114191	17/8	Hebrew. Cautious, guarded by God.
Serena First vowel E – to communicate	159551	26/8	Latin. Bright tranquil one.
Sheba First vowel E – to communicate	18521	17/8	Greek. Woman of Sheba.
Susanna First vowel U – to protect	1311551	17/8	Hebrew. Graceful lily.
Therese First vowel E – to communicate	2859515	35/8	Greek. The harvester.

Thora 28691 26/8
First vowel O – to study

Norse. Thunder from Thor.

Tina 2951 17/8
First vowel I – intuition

Latin. Dim. of Martina.

Virginia 49979591 53/8
First vowel I – intuition

Latin. Maidenly and pure.

Wendy 55547 26/8
First vowel E – to communicate

Teutonic. The wanderer.

Xena 6551 17/8
First vowel E – to communicate

Greek. Hospitality.

Yetta 75221 17/8
First vowel E – to communicate

Anglo-Saxon. To give, the giver. Also, dim. of Henrietta.

Zabrina 8129951 35/8
First vowel A – to lead

Anglo-Saxon. Noble maid.

Zelia 85391 26/8
First vowel E – to communicate

Greek. Zealous one.

Zerlinda 85939541 44/8
First vowel E – to communicate

Hebrew. Beautiful as the dawn.

NUMBER EIGHT NAMES – BOYS

Name	Number	Total	Origins and Meanings
Abraham First vowel A – to lead	1291814	26/8	Hebrew. Father of the multitudes.
Alaric First vowel A – to lead	131993	26/8	Teutonic. Ruler of all.
Alistair First vowel A – to lead	13912199	35/8	Greek. Derived from Alexander, 'helper and protector of mankind'.
Allen First vowel A – to lead	13355	17/8	Gaelic. Cheerful harmony.
Angus First vowel A – to lead	15731	17/8	Celtic. Outstanding.
Antony First vowel A – to lead	152657	26/8	Latin. Of inestimable worth.
Avery First vowel A – to lead	14597	26/8	Anglo-Saxon. Ruler of the elves.
Barrie First vowel A – to lead	219995	35/8	Gaelic. Spearlike.
Benedict First vowel E – to communicate	25554932	35/8	Latin. Blessed.
Bernard First vowel E – to communicate	2595194	35/8	Teutonic. As brave as a bear.
Bevan First vowel E – to communicate	25415	17/8	Welsh. Son of a nobleman.
Boaz First vowel O – to study	2618	17/8	Hebrew. 'In the Lord is strength'.
Braden First vowel A – to lead	291455	26/8	Anglo-Saxon. From the wide valley.
Brian First vowel I – intuition	29915	26/8	Celtic. Powerful strength with virtue and honour.
Brodie First vowel O – to study	296495	35/8	Gaelic. Ditch.

Brooks   296621   26/8
First vowel O – to study

Anglo-Saxon. One who lives by the brook.

Brough   296378   35/8
First vowel O – to study

Anglo-Saxon. The fortified residence.

Bryce   29735   26/8
First vowel E – to communicate

Celtic. Quick, ambitious, alert.

Casper   311759   26/8
First vowel A – to lead

Persian. Master of the treasure.

Chauncey   38135357   35/8
First vowel A – to lead

French. Chancellor.

Cole   3635   17/8
First vowel O – to study

Greek. Derived from Nicholas, 'the leader of the people'.

Colin   36395   26/8
First vowel O – to study

Gaelic. Strong and virile.

Cornelius   369553931   44/8
First vowel O – to study

Latin. Battle horn.

Crispian   39917915   44/8
First vowel I – intuition

Latin. Curly haired.

Curt   3392   17/8
First vowel U – to protect

French. The courteous one.

Dafydd   416744   26/8
First vowel A – to lead

Welsh form of the Hebrew David, 'the beloved one'.

Dudley   434357   26/8
First vowel U – to protect

Anglo-Saxon. From the people's meadow.

Eamonn   514655   26/8
First vowel E – to communicate

Anglo-Saxon. Rich guardian.

Eben   5255   17/8
First vowel E – to communicate

Hebrew. Stone.

Ebenezer   52555859   44/8
First vowel E – to communicate

Hebrew. Stone of help.

Edgar   54719   26/8
First vowel E – to communicate

Anglo-Saxon. Lucky spear warrior.

Eli   539   17/8
First vowel E – to communicate

Hebrew. The Highest.

Elvin   53495   26/8
First vowel E – to communicate

Anglo-Saxon. Noble and famous.

Name	Number	Total	Origins and Meanings
Emanuel	5415353	26/8	Hebrew. 'God is with us'.
First vowel E – to communicate			
Emrys	54971	26/8	Welsh form of Ambrose, 'belonging to the divine immortals'.
First vowel E – to communicate			
Eric	5993	26/8	Norse. All powerful ruler.
First vowel E – to communicate			
Farand	619154	26/8	Teutonic. Pleasant and attractive.
First vowel A – to lead			
Floyd	63674	26/8	Welsh. Grey haired.
First vowel O – to study			
Garrett	7199522	35/8	Anglo-Saxon. Mighty spear warrior.
First vowel A – to lead			
Gavin	71495	26/8	Celtic. The battle hawk.
First vowel A – to lead			
Gaynor	717569	35/8	Gaelic. Son of the blond haired one.
First vowel A – to lead			
Gerard	759194	35/8	Anglo-Saxon. Spear strong, spear brave.
First vowel E – to communicate			
Gerrard	7599194	44/8	Anglo-Saxon. Spear strong, spear brave.
First vowel E – to communicate			
Glendon	7355465	35/8	Celtic. From the glen's fortress.
First vowel E – to communicate			
Godfrey	7646957	44/8	Teutonic. God's divine peace.
First vowel O – to study			
Grahame	7918145	35/8	Teutonic. From the grey lands.
First vowel A – to lead			
Gregg	79577	35/8	Greek (Gregory). The watchful one.
First vowel E – to communicate			
Guy	737	17/8	French/Teutonic/Latin. Guide/warrior/life.
First vowel U – to protect			
Hugh	8378	26/8	Teutonic. Brilliant shining mind.
First vowel U – to protect			
Josiah	161918	26/8	Hebrew (Joseph). He shall add.
First vowel O – to study			
Justis	131291	17/8	French. Justice, strict upholder of morals.
First vowel U – to protect			

Keith	25928	26/8	Celtic. A place, or from the forest.
First vowel E – to communicate			
Kenn	2555	17/8	Celtic. Clear bright water.
First vowel E – to communicate			
Kenrick	2559932	35/8	Anglo-Saxon. Bold ruler.
First vowel E – to communicate			
Kyle	2735	17/8	Gaelic. From the strait.
First vowel E – to communicate			
Lance	31535	17/8	French. Spear attendant.
First vowel A – to lead			
Lauren	313955	26/8	Latin. Crowned with laurels.
First vowel A – to lead			
Leslie	351395	26/8	Celtic. From the grey fort.
First vowel E – to communicate			
Liam	3914	17/8	Teutonic. Determined protector.
First vowel I – intuition			
Lyall	37133	17/8	French. From the island.
First vowel A – to lead			
Mac	413	8	Celtic, Irish, Scots, meaning son.
First vowel A – to lead			
Malvin	413495	26/8	Celtic. Polished chief.
First vowel A – to lead			
Marc	4193	17/8	Latin. Follower of Mars.
First vowel A – to lead			
Mason	41165	17/8	Latin. Worker in stone.
First vowel A – to lead			
Mayer	41759	26/8	Latin. Greater.
First vowel A – to lead			
Merlin	459395	35/8	Anglo-Saxon. The falcon.
First vowel E – to communicate			
Moses	46151	17/8	Hebrew. Saved from the water.
First vowel O – to study			
Neall	55133	17/8	Gaelic. The champion.
First vowel E – to communicate			
Nicol	59363	26/8	Greek (Nicholas). Leader of the people.
First vowel I – intuition			
Osmond	614654	26/8	Anglo-Saxon. Divine protector.
First vowel O – to study			

Name	Number	Total	Origins and Meanings
Owain First vowel O – to study	65195	26/8	Celtic. The young, well born warrior.
Perrie First vowel E – to communicate	759995	44/8	Anglo-Saxon. From the pear tree. Also dim. of Peregrine.
Quincy First vowel I – intuition	839537	35/8	French/Latin. From the fifth son of the estate.
Randall First vowel A – to lead	9154133	26/8	Old English. Shield wolf.
Ray First vowel A – to lead	917	17/8	French. The sovereign.
Rob First vowel O – to study	962	17/8	Teutonic. Derived from Robert, 'bright, shining fame'.
Ronan First vowel O – to study	96515	26/8	Gaelic. Little seal.
Ross First vowel O – to study	9611	17/8	Celtic. From the peninsula.
Royd First vowel O – to study	9674	26/8	Norse. From the forest clearing.
Rupert First vowel U – to protect	937592	35/8	Teutonic. Bright shining fame.
Salomon First vowel A – to lead	1136465	26/8	Hebrew. Wise and peaceful.
Samuel First vowel A – to lead	114353	17/8	Hebrew. 'His name is God'.
Sanders First vowel A – to lead	1154591	26/8	Anglo-Saxon. Son of Alexander.
Saul First vowel A – to lead	1133	8	Hebrew. Called by God.
Selwyn First vowel E – to communicate	153575	26/8	Teutonic. Friend of the manor house.
Spence First vowel E – to communicate	175535	26/8	French. Shopkeeper, dispenser of goods.
Spencer First vowel E – to communicate	1755359	35/8	French. Shopkeeper, dispenser of goods.

Tavis   21491   17/8
First vowel A – to lead

Celtic. Son of David.

Theon   28565   26/8
First vowel E – to communicate

Greek. Godly man.

Theron   285965   35/8
First vowel E – to communicate

Greek. The hunter.

Thorne   286955   35/8
First vowel O – to study

Anglo-Saxon. From the thorn tree.

Timon   29465   26/8
First vowel I – intuition

Greek. Honour, reward, value.

Toby   2627   17/8
First vowel O – to study

Hebrew. 'God is good'.

Travis   291491   26/8
First vowel A – to lead

Latin. From the crossroads.

Trevor   295469   35/8
First vowel E – to communicate

Gaelic. Prudent, wise, discreet.

Tyler   27359   26/8
First vowel E – to communicate

Anglo-Saxon. Maker of tiles and bricks.

Vail   4193   17/8
First vowel A – to lead

Anglo-Saxon. From the valley.

Verney   459557   35/8
First vowel E – to communicate

French. From the alder grove.

Wat   512   8
First vowel A – to lead

Teutonic. Mighty warrior.

Wesley   551357   26/8
First vowel E – to communicate

Anglo-Saxon. From the west meadow.

Wyatt   57122   17/8
First vowel A – to lead

French. The guide.

Yves   7451   17/8
First vowel E – to communicate

French form of Ives, son of the archer.

NUMBER NINE QUALITIES

If your birth number reduces to a Nine you have the ability to energise, capitalise and utilise. There can be great creative or destructive energy in a Nine. It is up to you to harness, direct or project this energy to the full.

Many famous people who excel in sports or combative careers have Nine as a birth number. A Nine is at his best when under stress, living off his wits, mental energy and guile. Inactivity is the ruin of a Nine, so he should avoid criminal activities as jail would be too claustrophobic for him.

Soldiers, sportsmen and adventurers of all types are the ruling Nines that occupy our world. Nines need to learn to harness their energy to one task at a time and avoid being sidetracked. In this way they may achieve the stability that the number sometimes lacks. If you were born a Nine, you were given the energy to succeed; all you need now is the patience to apply that energy to the task in hand.

Nines get on best with other Nines, Sixes or Threes.

Any number of this vibration will strengthen the birth number and your child's personality. Or choose one of the three directional numbers (pp. 7–8).

TYPES OF NINES

18/9   blends leadership and maturity with energy. A Nine of this type will not tolerate orders or close supervision. The freedom to express ideals and ambitions through their own creativity is a must for this number. This Nine should avoid restrictive environments and strive for self-sufficiency.

27/9   Compassion and imagination coupled with the will to succeed; this can best express itself through group activities. This type of Nine would make a great actor, being able to adapt to whatever environment or circumstances he finds himself in. He does, however, require reassurance for a job well done.

36/9   If this Nine was not so complacent at times, he could go right to the top. However, he tends to operate in spurts of activity followed by periods of inactivity. Creative and home-loving at heart, this Nine should not make promises he cannot keep.

45/9   Security and communication blend well for this type of Nine. He must, however, learn to make allowances for those around him; he can be very impatient with those who fail to keep pace with him. He must also reorganise his inner motives for what he does.

54/9   This Nine is very hard to tie down — here today and gone tomorrow could be his adage. He must endeavour to complete one task at a time rather than half finishing many. This is, however, a good active number for a soldier of fortune.

63/9   Not known to us as a name number.

NUMBER NINE NAMES – GIRLS

Name	Number	Total	Origins and Meanings
Adele First vowel A – to lead	14535	18/9	Teutonic. Noble and kind.
Alda First vowel A – to lead	1341	9	Teutonic. Wise and rich.
Alima First vowel A – to lead	13941	18/9	Arabic. Learned in music and dancing.
Alma First vowel A – to lead	1341	9	Latin. Cherishing spirit.
Almira First vowel A – to lead	134991	27/9	Arabic. Truth without question.
Alva First vowel A – to lead	1341	9	Latin. White lady.
Angelina First vowel A – to lead	15753951	36/9	Greek. Heavenly messenger.
Angharad First vowel A – to lead	15781914	36/9	Welsh. Free from shame.
Anita First vowel A – to lead	15921	18/9	Hebrew. Grace (form of Anne).
Anona First vowel A– to lead	15651	18/9	Latin. Yearly crops, the Roman goddess of crops.
Areta First vowel A – to lead	19521	18/9	Greek. Of excellent virtue.
Augusta First vowel A – to lead	1373121	18/9	Latin. Sacred and majestic.
Beatrice First vowel E – to communicate	25129935	36/9	Latin. She who brings joy.
Belle First vowel E – to communicate	25335	18/9	French. Beautiful woman.
Benedicta First vowel E – to communicate	255549321	36/9	Latin. Blessed one.
Bertha First vowel E – to communicate	259281	27/9	Teutonic. Bright and shining.

Blanche 2315385 27/9 French. Fair and white.
First vowel A – to lead

Bronwyn 2965575 39/9 Welsh/Celtic. From the
First vowel O – to study thicket. Fem. of Bruce.

Bryony 297657 36/9 Old. English. A twining
First vowel O – to study vine.

Candida 3154941 27/9 Latin. Pure white.
First vowel A – to lead

Carmen 319455 27/9 Latin. Songstress,
First vowel A – to lead clear-voiced.

Carole 319635 27/9 Teutonic. Little woman,
First vowel A – to lead born to command.

Catriona 31299651 36/9 Greek (Catherine). Pure
First vowel A – to lead maiden.

Ceiridwen 359994555 54/9 Welsh. Goddess of
First vowel E – to communicate bards.

Charmaine 381941955 45/9 Latin. Little song.
First vowel A – to lead

Dacia 41391 18/9 Greek. From Dacia.
First vowel A – to lead

Deidre 459495 36/9 Gaelic. Sorrow.
First vowel E – to communicate

Deirdre 4599495 45/9 Gaelic. Sorrow.
First vowel E – to communicate

Dextra 456291 27/9 Latin. Skilful, adept.
First vowel E – to communicate

Dinah 49518 27/9 Hebrew. Judgment in
First vowel I – intuition understanding.

Dulcie 433395 27/9 Latin. Sweet and
First vowel U – to protect charming.

Elberta 5325921 27/9 Teutonic. Noble and
First vowel E – to communicate brilliant.

Elisabeth 539112528 36/9 Hebrew. Consecrated to
First vowel E – to communicate God.

Elvina 534951 27/9 Anglo-Saxon. Friend of
First vowel E – to communicate the elves.

Erica 59931 27/9 Norse. Powerful ruler.
First vowel E – to communicate

Name	Number	Total	Origins and Meanings
Eveline	5453955	36/9	Hebrew. Life giver.
First vowel E – to communicate			
Felicia	6539391	36/9	Latin. Joyous one.
First vowel E – to communicate			
Fernanda	65951541	36/9	Teutonic. Adventurous.
First vowel E – to communicate			
Fiona	69651	27/9	Gaelic. Fair one.
First vowel I – intuition			
Germaine	75941955	45/9	French. From Germany.
First vowel E – to communicate			
Gwenda	755541	27/9	Celtic. White browed maid.
First vowel E – to communicate			
Gwendolen	755546355	45/9	Celtic. Whited browed maid.
First vowel E – to communicate			
Gwendoline	7555463955	54/9	Celtic. White browed maid.
First vowel E – to communicate			
Helena	853551	27/9	Greek. Light.
First vowel E – to communicate			
Holly	86337	27/9	Anglo-Saxon. Bringer of good luck.
First vowel O – to study			
Horatia	8691291	36/9	Latin. Keeper of the hours.
First vowel O – to study			
Inez	9558	27/9	Greek (Agnes). Pure, chaste, lamblike.
First vowel I – intuition			
Jacquelyn	113835375	36/9	Hebrew. The supplanter.
First vowel A – to lead			
Jennifer	15559659	45/9	Celtic. White phantom.
First vowel E – to communicate			
Joann	16155	18/9	Hebrew (Jane). God's gift of grace.
First vowel O – to study			
Johanna	1681551	27/9	Hebrew. God's gift of grace.
First vowel O – to study			
Jody	1647	18/9	Hebrew (Judith). Admired and praised.
First vowel O – to study			
Jordana	1694151	27/9	Hebrew. Descending.
First vowel O – to study			

Judith First vowel U – to protect	134928	27/9	Hebrew. Admired and praised.
Levina First vowel E – to communicate	354951	27/9	English. The bright flash.
Lilli First vowel I – intuition	39339	27/9	Latin. A lily.
Linnette First vowel I – intuition	39555225	36/9	French. Sweet bird.
Louise First vowel O – to study	363915	27/9	Teutonic. Famous battle maid.
Luella First vowel U – to protect	335331	18/9	Anglo-Saxon. The appeaser.
Madeline First vowel A – to lead	41453955	36/9	Greek. Tower of strength.
Malvina First vowel A – to lead	4134951	27/9	Gaelic. Polished chieftain.
Marcia First vowel A – to lead	419391	27/9	Latin. Belonging to Mars.
Marguerite First vowel A – to lead	4197359925	54/9	Latin. A pearl.
Marla First vowel A – to lead	41931	18/9	Greek (Madeline). Tower of strength.
Mercedes First vowel E – to communicate	45935451	36/9	Spanish. Compassionate, merciful.
Miriam First vowel I – intuition	499914	36/9	Hebrew (Mary). Bitterness.
Morag First vowel O – to study	46917	27/9	Celtic. Great.
Moyra First vowel O – to study	46791	27/9	Celtic. Great.
Musetta First vowel U – to protect	4315221	18/9	French. Child of the Muses.
Nelda First vowel E – to communicate	55341	18/9	Anglo-Saxon. Born under an elder tree.
Nicola First vowel I – intuition	593631	27/9	Greek. Leader of the people.

Name	Number	Total	Origins and Meanings
Noelle	565335	27/9	French. Born at
First vowel O – to study			Christmas time.
Odessa	645111	18/9	Greek. Long journey.
First vowel O – to study			
Olive	63945	27/9	Latin. Olive tree,
First vowel O – to study			symbol of peace.
Oona	6651	18/9	Latin. One.
First vowel O – to study			
Ottilie	6229395	36/9	Teutonic. Prosperous
First vowel O – to study			one.
Perina	759951	36/9	Greek. Steadfast as a
First vowel E – to communicate			rock.
Priscilla	799139331	45/9	Latin. Of ancient
First vowel I – intuition			lineage.
Prospera	79617591	45/9	Latin. Favourable.
First vowel O – to study			
Prunella	79355331	36/9	French. Plum coloured.
First vowel U – to protect			
Queena	835551	27/9	Teutonic. The queen,
First vowel U – to protect			supreme ruler.
Regina	957951	36/9	Latin. Queen. Born to
First vowel E – to communicate			rule.
Rexana	956151	27/9	Latin. Regal, graceful.
First vowel E – to communicate			
Roanna	961551	27/9	Latin. Sweet and
First vowel O – to study			gracious.
Rosabel	9611253	27/9	Latin. Beautiful rose.
First vowel O – to study			
Rosamond	96114654	36/9	French. Rose of the
First vowel O – to study			world.
Samuela	1143531	18/9	Hebrew. Fem. of
First vowel A – to lead			Samuel, 'His name is God'.
Sheila	185931	27/9	Celtic. Musical.
First vowel E – to communicate			
Silvia	193491	27/9	Latin. From the forest.
First vowel I – intuition			

Sophie	167895	36/9	Greek. Wisdom.
First vowel O – to study			
Tamara	214191	18/9	Hebrew. Palm tree.
First vowel A – to lead			
Tammy	21447	18/9	Hebrew. Perfection.
First vowel A – to lead			
Tania	21591	18/9	Russian. The fairy queen.
First vowel A – to lead			
Thyra	28791	27/9	Greek. Shield bearer.
First vowel A – to lead			
Tracey	291357	27/9	Gaelic. Battler.
First vowel A – to lead			
Una	351	9	Latin. One.
First vowel U – to protect			
Vala	4131	9	Teutonic. The chosen one.
First vowel A – to lead			
Valerie	4135995	36/9	French. Strong.
First vowel A – to lead			
Vanessa	4155111	18/9	Greek. The butterfly.
First vowel A – to lead			
Venus	45531	18/9	Latin. Loveliness, Goddess of Love.
First vowel E – to communicate			
Vicki	49329	27/9	Latin (Victoria). The victorious one.
First vowel I – intuition			
Vivien	494955	36/9	Latin. Alive.
First vowel I – intuition			
Vonny	46557	27/9	Latin (Veronica). True image.
First vowel O – to study			
Wynne	57555	27/9	Celtic. Fair white maiden.
First vowel E – to communicate			
Xanthe	615285	27/9	Greek. Golden blonde.
First vowel A – to lead			
Zenobia	8556291	36/9	Greek. 'Zeus gave life'.
First vowel E – to communicate			
Zetta	85221	18/9	Anglo-Saxon. Sixth born.
First vowel E – to communicate			
Zeva	8541	18/9	Greek. Sword.
First vowel E – to communicate			

NUMBER NINE NAMES – BOYS

Name	Number	Total	Origins and Meanings
Alastair First vowel A – to lead	13112199	27/9	Greek (Alexander). Helper and protector of mankind.
Aldis First vowel A – to lead	13491	18/9	Anglo-Saxon. From the old house.
Aldous First vowel A – to lead	134631	18/9	Anglo-Saxon. From the old house.
Alphonse First vowel A – to lead	13786515	36/9	Teutonic. Noble and ready.
Amory First vowel A – to lead	14697	27/9	Teutonic. Famous ruler.
Arney First vowel A – to lead	19557	27/9	Teutonic. The eagle.
Ashlin First vowel A – to lead	118395	27/9	Anglo-Saxon. Dweller by the ash tree pool.
Aubrey First vowel A – to lead	132957	27/9	Teutonic. Elf ruler, golden haired king.
Audwin First vowel A – to lead	134595	27/9	Teutonic. Noble friend.
Barnaby First vowel A – to lead	2195127	27/9	Hebrew. Son of consolation.
Bert First vowel E – to communicate	2592	18/9	Anglo-Saxon. Bright raven.
Bogart First vowel O – to study	267192	27/9	Teutonic. Strong bow.
Boris First vowel O – to study	26991	27/9	Slavonic. A fighter, born warrior.
Burton First vowel U – to protect	239265	27/9	Anglo-Saxon. Of bright and glorious fame.
Caradoc First vowel A – to lead	3191463	27/9	Celtic. Beloved.
Cain First vowel A – to lead	3195	18/9	Hebrew. The possessed.

Chase 38115 18/9 French. The hunter.
First vowel A – to lead

Cian 3915 18/9 Gaelic. The ancient
First vowel I – intuition one, long life.

Clark 33192 18/9 French. Wise and
First vowel A – to lead learned scholar.

Clayton 3317265 27/9 Anglo-Saxon. From clay
First vowel A – to lead town, or mortal man.

Clement 3354552 27/9 Latin. Kind and
First vowel E – to communicate merciful.

Cliff 33966 27/9 Anglo-Saxon. From the
First vowel I – intuition ford by the hills.

Colley 363357 27/9 Greek. Derived from
First vowel O – to study Nicholas, 'leader of the
people'.

Conal 36513 18/9 Celtic. High and
First vowel O – to study mighty.

Conroy 365967 36/9 Gaelic. The wise one.
First vowel O – to study

Cormick 3694932 36/9 Gaelic. Charioteer.
First vowel O – to study

Curtis 339291 27/9 French. The courteous
First vowel U – to protect one.

Cynric 375993 36/9 Anglo-Saxon. From the
First vowel I – intuition royal line of kings.

Daniel 415953 27/9 Hebrew. 'God is my
First vowel A – to lead judge'.

Darius 419931 27/9 Greek. The wealthy
First vowel A – to lead man.

Devin 45495 27/9 Gaelic. The poet.
First vowel E – to communicate

Dugal 43713 18/9 Celtic. From the dark
First vowel U – to protect stream.

Dwayne 451755 27/9 Gaelic, small dark man.
First vowel A – to lead Celtic, the singer.

Earl 5193 18/9 Anglo-Saxon.
First vowel E – to communicate Nobleman, chief.

Name	Number	Total	Origins and Meanings
Egan First vowel E – to communicate	5715	18/9	Gaelic. Formidable, fiery.
Elmo First vowel E – to communicate	5346	18/9	Italian/Greek. Protector/friendly.
Enoch First vowel E – to communicate	55638	27/9	Hebrew. Consecrated, dedicated, devoted.
Ernest First vowel E – to communicate	595512	27/9	Anglo-Saxon. Sincere and earnest.
Erskine First vowel E – to communicate	5912955	36/9	Celtic. From the cliff's height.
Ewald First vowel E – to communicate	55134	18/9	Anglo-Saxon. Law, powerful.
Farquhar First vowel A – to lead	61983819	45/9	Gaelic. Friendly man.
Fidel First vowel I – intuition	69453	27/9	Latin. Advocate of the poor.
Filmer First vowel I – intuition	693459	36/9	Anglo-Saxon. Very famous one.
Fitzgerald First vowel I – intuition	6928759134	54/9	Anglo-Saxon. Son of Gerald.
Fredric First vowel E – to communicate	6954993	45/9	Teutonic. Peaceful ruler.
Gabriel First vowel A – to lead	7129953	36/9	Hebrew. Messenger of God.
Gable First vowel A – to lead	71235	18/9	French. The small Gabriel.
Garth First vowel A – to lead	71928	27/9	Norse. From the garden.
Gervais First vowel E – to communicate	7594191	36/9	Teutonic. Spear vassal.
Gideon First vowel E – to communicate	794565	36/9	Hebrew. Brave indomitable spirit.
Godwin First vowel O – to study	764595	36/9	Anglo-Saxon. Good friend.
Gorden First vowel O – to study	769455	36/9	Anglo-Saxon. From the cornered hill.

Hogan   86715   27/9   Celtic. Youth.
First vowel O – to study

Holmes   863451   27/9   Anglo-Saxon. From the
First vowel O – to study   island in the river.

Hudson   834165   27/9   Anglo-Saxon. Son of
First vowel U – to protect   the hoodsman.

Irvin   99495   36/9   Anglo-Saxon. Sea
First vowel I – intuition   friend.

Jay   117   9   Anglo-Saxon. Jay or
First vowel A – to lead   crow.

Job   162   9   Hebrew. The
First vowel O – to study   persecuted or afflicted.

Keneth   255528   27/9   Celtic. The handsome.
First vowel E – to communicate

Kenley   255357   27/9   Anglo-Saxon. Owner of
First vowel E – to communicate   the royal meadow.

Konrad   265914   27/9   Teutonic. Brave
First vowel O – to study   counsellor.

Lamar   31419   18/9   Teutonic. Famous
First vowel A – to lead   throughout the land.

Lander   315459   27/9   Anglo-Saxon. Owner of
First vowel A – to lead   the grassland.

Lawrence   31595535   36/9   Latin. Crowned with
First vowel A – to lead   laurels.

Leith   35928   27/9   Celtic. Broad wide river.
First vowel E – to communicate

Litton   392265   27/9   Anglo-Saxon. From the
First vowel I – intuition   farm on the hillside.

Lyle   3735   18/9   French. From the
First vowel E – to communicate   island.

Madoc   41463   18/9   Welsh. Fortunate.
First vowel A – to lead

Malachy   4131387   27/9   Irish form of Andrew.
First vowel A – to lead

Marius   419931   27/9   Latin. The martial one.
First vowel A – to lead

Matthew   4122855   27/9   Hebrew. Gift of God.
First vowel A – to lead

Name	Number	Total	Origins and Meanings
Maxwell First vowel A – to lead	4165533	27/9	Anglo-Saxon. Large spring.
Mayo First vowel A – to lead	4176	18/9	Gaelic. From the plain of the yew trees.
Mervin First vowel E – to communicate	459495	36/9	Anglo-Saxon. Famous friend.
Nicholas First vowel I – intuition	59386311	36/9	Greek. Victorious army, leader of the people.
Ogden First vowel O – to study	67455	27/9	Anglo-Saxon. From the oak valley.
Oliver First vowel O – to study	639459	36/9	Latin. The olive tree, symbol of peace.
Orson First vowel O – to study	69165	27/9	Latin. Little bear.
Phineas First vowel I – intuition	7895511	36/9	Greek. Mouth of brass.
Ranulf First vowel A – to lead	915336	27/9	Old English. Shield wolf.
Raymond First vowel A – to lead	9174654	36/9	Teutonic. Wise protection.
Reece First vowel E – to communicate	95535	27/9	Celtic. The ardent one.
Regan First vowel E – to communicate	95715	27/9	Gaelic. Royalty, a king.
Ritchie First vowel I – intuition	9923895	45/9	Teutonic (Richard). Wealthy and powerful.
Robertson First vowel O – to study	962592165	45/9	Teutonic. Son of Robert.
Roderic First vowel O – to study	9645993	45/9	Teutonic. Famous, wealthy ruler.
Rodney First vowel O – to study	964557	36/9	Teutonic. Famous and renowned.
Roger First vowel O – to study	96759	36/9	Teutonic. Famous spearman.
Rutland First vowel U – to protect	9323154	27/9	Norse. From the stump land.

Sabin	11295	18/9	Latin. Man of the
First vowel A – to lead			Sabine tribe.
Samson	114165	18/9	Hebrew. Sun's man.
First vowel A – to lead			
Sandy	11547	18/9	Greek (Alexander).
First vowel A – to lead			Helper and protector of
			mankind.
Sebastian	152112915	27/9	Latin. Reverenced,
First vowel E – to communicate			august one.
Sextus	156231	18/9	Latin. Sixth born.
First vowel E – to communicate			
Shamus	181431	18/9	Hebrew (James).
First vowel A – to lead			The supplanter.
Shaun	18135	18/9	Irish form of John.
First vowel A – to lead			
Slevin	135495	27/9	Gaelic. The mountain
First vowel E – to communicate			climber.
Sterne	125955	27/9	Anglo-Saxon. The
First vowel E – to communicate			austere one.
Stirling	12993957	45/9	Teutonic. Good,
First vowel I – intuition			honest, Celtic, from the
			yellow house.
Stuart	123192	18/9	Anglo-Saxon. The
First vowel U – to protect			steward.
Theodore	29564695	45/9	Greek. Gift of God.
First vowel E – to communicate			
Vance	41535	18/9	Anglo-Saxon. From the
First vowel A – to lead			grain barn.
Vivien	494955	36/9	Latin. Lively one.
First vowel I – intuition			
Wilfrid	5936994	45/9	Teutonic. Firm peace
First vowel I – intuition			maker.
Yehudi	758349	36/9	Hebrew. 'Praise to the
First vowel E – to communicate			Lord'.

UNDERSTANDING MASTER NUMBERS

In numerology there have always been numbers that are considered to be a cut above the rest, namely the numbers 11, 22 and 33. It is said that he who uses these numbers on their higher spiritual plane will have a special task to perform. These numbers should not be reduced to their base numbers but operated on their higher plane.

Why the first three multiples of 11 were used (some even include 10) has never been fully explained, but suffice it to say they are.

If you reduce certain names and words in the English language, it may be found that they reduce to some of these numbers. For example, the word 'Saviour' becomes 1+1+4+9+6+3+9=33. The word 'Jesus' becomes 1+5+1+3+1=11. The word 'authority' becomes 1+3+2+8+6+9+9+2+7=11. And so on and so on.

11 as a Master Number is the lower vibration of 33 and it is said that those with the number 11 as a major vibration are thought to be reincarnated souls whose mission in this life is to lead their fellow man to higher levels through inspiration and the subconscious knowledge of previous existences. As it is a higher form of 2, it is the transition from material to spiritual partnerships, the body and soul working together as one. Some allow the number 11 when it comes from reduced 29, 38, 47, 56, 65, etc. I feel that if it is to have any real force it should be a straight 11 as in the name BEATA = 25121 = 11/2, for in this form it is at its strongest, undiluted and untainted by other numbers.

The number 22 is the second Master Number and is considered to be master of the material and spiritual planes. Those born with 22 as a birth number are thought to possess power to build strong corporations, societies and charities of the world for the betterment of mankind. Such people are said to have mastered the physical and, in so doing, have it to command. Those with this number are also said to come before the people in some way, ideally as leaders; on the negative side however, there is infamy. If your date of birth or name number is a straight 22, it is not reduced and you must learn to accept and shoulder the physical responsibilities for your fellow man.

The last Master Number is 33, which is made by the forces of 11 and 22 combining to the superior level of the Saviour. Those with this number strong in date of birth or name have an enormous weight placed upon them, as it is through their own self-sacrifice and devotion, both physically (22) and spiritually (11), that they must endeavour to save mankind.

As you may appreciate, this is a task that saints can barely live up to. As few are able to maintain the life of selfless devotion imposed upon the higher 33, most revert to the 6 and become lovers and admirers of the Arts and literature in some form.

So, before you choose a Master Number name for a baby, think carefully; you may be giving your child higher responsibilities than they may care to shoulder in later life.

NUMBER 11 NAMES — GIRLS

Name	Number	Total	Origins and Meanings
Alana First vowel A – to lead	13151	11	Celtic. Bright fair one.
Alula First vowel A – to lead	13331	11	Latin, winged one, Arabic, the first.
Ara First vowel A – to lead	191	11	Greek. Spirit of revenge.
Beata First vowel E – to communicate	25121	11	Latin. Blessed or divine one.
Calla First vowel A – to lead	31331	11	Greek. Beautiful.
Dana First vowel A – to lead	4151	·11	Anglo-Saxon. From Denmark.
Ena First vowel E – to communicate	551	11	Gaelic. Little ardent one.
Ira First vowel I – intuition	911	11	Teutonic. Lady of iron.
Jade First vowel A – to lead	1145	11	Spanish. Daughter, a mother's best jewel.
Leta First vowel E – to communicate	3521	11	Latin. Joyous gladness.
Susan First vowel U – to protect	13115	11	Hebrew. Graceful lily.
Ulva First vowel U – to protect	3341	11	Teutonic. The she wolf, bravery.

NUMBER 11 NAMES — BOYS

Name	Number	Total	Origins and Meanings
Abel First vowel A – to lead	1253	11	Hebrew. Breath. First murder victim.
Beal First vowel E – to communicate	2513	11	French. Handsome.
Beau First vowel E – to communicate	2513	11	French. Handsome, smart.
Black First vowel A – to lead	23132	11	Anglo-Saxon. Of dark complexion.
Claus First vowel A – to lead	33131	11	Greek (Nicholas). Leader of the people.
Lucas First vowel U – to protect	33311	11	Latin. Light.
Max First vowel A – to lead	416	11	Latin. The greatest.
Tadd First vowel A – to lead	2144	11	Celtic. Father.

NUMBER 22 NAMES – GIRLS

Name	Number	Total	Origins and Meanings
Alcina First vowel A – to lead	133951	22	Greek. Strong minded one.
Aminta First vowel A – to lead	149521	22	Greek. Protector.
Anastasia First vowel A – to lead	151121191	22	Greek. She who will rise again.
Angela First vowel A – to lead	157531	22	Greek. Heavenly messenger.
Annabel First vowel A – to lead	1551253	22	Combination of Anna and Belle.
Anora First vowel A – to lead	15691	22	English. Light and graceful.
Anthea First vowel A – to lead	152851	22	Greek. Flower-like.
Athena First vowel A – to lead	128551	22	Greek. The Greek goddess of wisdom.
Azura First vowel A – to lead	18391	22	French. The blue sky.
Beulah First vowel E – to communicate	253318	22	Hebrew. The married one.
Blyth No vowel, I sound	23728	22	Anglo-Saxon. Joyful and happy.
Brena First vowel E – to communicate	29551	22	Irish. Raven-haired beauty.
Candace First vowel A – to lead	3154135	22	Latin. Pure, brilliant white.
Columba First vowel O – to study	3633421	22	Latin. The dove, one of peace.
Coral First vowel O – to study	36913	22	Latin. Sincere, from the sea.
Daisy First vowel A – to lead	41917	22	Anglo-Saxon. The day's eye.

Name	Number		Origin and meaning
Darel	41953	22	Anglo-Saxon. Little dear one.
First vowel A – to lead			
Delia	45391	22	Greek. Visible. Moon goddess.
First vowel E – to communicate			
Doanna	461551	22	Combination of Dorothy and Anne.
First vowel O – to study			
Dyane	47155	22	Latin. The Moon goddess.
First vowel A – to lead			
Fonda	66541	22	English. Affectionate.
First vowel O – to study			
Garda	71941	22	Norse. Protected one.
First vowel A – to lead			
Gina	7951	22	Latin (Regina)/Greek (Eugenia). Queen/ Woman of noble family.
First vowel I – intuition			
Gwen	7555	22	Celtic. White browed maiden.
First vowel E – to communicate			
Hedda	85441	22	Teutonic. A born fighter.
First vowel E – to communicate			
Iduna	94351	22	Norse. Lover, keeper of youth.
First vowel I – intuition			
Josette	1615225	22	Hebrew. 'She shall add'. Fem. of Joseph.
First vowel O – to study			
Joyce	16735	22	Latin. Gay and joyful.
First vowel O – to study			
Juanita	1315921	22	Hebrew. God's gift of grace.
First vowel U – to protect			
Justina	1312951	22	Latin. The just one.
First vowel U – to protect			
Karen	21955	22	Greek. Pure maiden.
First vowel A – to lead			
Keely	25537	22	Gaelic. The beautiful one.
First vowel E – to communicate			
Lily	3937	22	Latin. Lily flower.
First vowel I – intuition			
Linda	39541	22	Spanish. Pretty one.
First vowel I – intuition			

Name	Number	Total	Origins and Meanings
Ludella First vowel U – to protect	3345331	22	Anglo-Saxon. Pixie maid.
Manuela First vowel A – to lead	4153531	22	Spanish. 'God with us.'
Megan First vowel E – to communicate	45715	22	Celtic. The strong.
Noleta First vowel O – to study	563521	22	Latin. Unwilling.
Paloma First vowel A – to lead	713641	22	Spanish. The dove.
Ruth First vowel U – to protect	9328	22	Hebrew. Compassionate and beautiful.
Secunda First vowel E – to communicate	1533541	22	Latin. Second born.
Sibyl First vowel I – intuition	19273	22	Greek. Prophetess.
Sonia First vowel O – to study	16591	22	Greek. Wisdom.
Starr First vowel A – to lead	12199	22	English. A star.
Storm First vowel O – to study	12694	22	Anglo-Saxon. A storm.
Sybil First vowel I – intuition	17293	22	Greek. Prophetess.
Tamsin First vowel A – to lead	214195	22	Hebrew. The twin.
Toni First vowel O – to study	2659	22	Latin (Antonia). Beyond price.
Tracy First vowel A – to lead	29137	22	Gaelic. Battler.
Wilma First vowel I – intuition	59341	22	Teutonic. The protectress.

NUMBER 22 NAMES – BOYS

Name	Number	Total	Origins and Meanings
Aaron First vowel A – to lead	11965	22	Hebrew. Exalted, brother of Moses.
Abner First vowel A – to lead	12559	22	Hebrew. Father of light.
Adler First vowel A – to lead	14359	22	Teutonic. Eagle.
Adney First vowel A – to lead	14557	22	Anglo-Saxon. Dweller on the island.
Aiken First vowel A – to lead	19255	22	Anglo-Saxon. Little Adam.
Albert First vowel A – to lead	132592	22	Teutonic. Noble and illustrious.
Alder First vowel A – to lead	13459	22	Anglo-Saxon. The alder tree.
Alonso First vowel A – to lead	136516	22	Teutonic. Noble and ready.
Alvin First vowel A – to lead	13495	22	Teutonic. Friend of all.
Ansley First vowel A – to lead	151357	22	Anglo-Saxon. From Ann's meadow.
Annell First vowel A – to lead	155533	22	Celtic. Beloved one.
Aric First vowel A – to lead	1993	22	Anglo-Saxon. Sacred ruler.
Arnall First vowel A – to lead	195133	22	Teutonic. Gracious eagle.
Aubert First vowel A – to lead	132592	22	Teutonic. Noble and illustrious.
Avenall First vowel A – to lead	1455133	22	French. Dweller in the oat field.
Barnabas First vowel A – to lead	21951211	22	Hebrew. Son of consolation.

Name	Number	Total	Origins and Meanings
Boden First vowel O – to study	26455	22	French. The herald, bringer of news.
Brock First vowel O – to study	29632	22	Anglo-Saxon. The badger.
Bruce First vowel U – to protect	29335	22	French. From the thicket.
Carol First vowel A – to lead	31963	22	Gaelic. The champion, unbeatable.
Carr First vowel A – to lead	3199	22	Norse. He who dwells by the marsh.
Caspar First vowel A – to lead	311719	22	Persian. Master of the Treasure.
Castor First vowel A – to lead	311269	22	Greek. The beaver, industrious.
Clint First vowel I – intuition	33952	22	Anglo-Saxon (Clinton). From the farm on the headland.
Clyde First vowel E – to communicate	33745	22	Celtic. Warm. Heard from afar.
Cullen First vowel U – to protect	333355	22	Gaelic. Handsome one.
David First vowel A – to lead	41494	22	Hebrew. The beloved one.
Dugald First vowel U – to protect	437134	22	Celtic. From the dark stream.
Edwald First vowel E – to communicate	545134	22	Anglo-Saxon. Prosperous ruler.
Elvis First vowel E – to communicate	53491	22	Norse. All wise, prince of wisdom.
Erastus First vowel E – to communicate	5911231	22	Greek. The beloved.
Erle First vowel E – to communicate	5935	22	Anglo-Saxon. Nobleman, chief.
Gaston First vowel A – to lead	711265	22	French. Man of Gascony.
Gene First vowel E – to communicate	7555	22	Greek (Eugene). Nobly born.

Glyn   7375   22   Celtic. From the valley.
No vowel, I sound

Jotham   162814   22   Hebrew. God is perfect.
First vowel O – to study

Julian   133915   22   Latin. Youthful.
First vowel U – to protect

Junius   135931   22   Latin. Born in June.
First vowel U – to protect

Kirk   2992   22   Norse. Dweller by the
First vowel I – intuition   church.

Louis   36391   22   Teutonic. Famous
First vowel O – to study   battle warrior.

Lucius   333931   22   Latin. Light.
First vowel U – to protect

Lundy   33547   22   French. Born on
First vowel U – to protect   Monday.

Malin   41395   22   Anglo-Saxon. Little
First vowel A – to lead   warrior.

Mandel   415453   22   Teutonic. Almond.
First vowel A – to lead

Miles   49351   22   Latin. Soldier.
First vowel I – intuition

Milo   4936   22   Latin. The miller.
First vowel I – intuition

Nathan   512815   22   Hebrew. Gift of God.
First vowel A – to lead

Neil   5593   22   Gaelic. The champion.
First vowel E – to communicate

Paget   71752   22   French. A page.
First vowel A – to lead

Raff   9166   22   Anglo-Saxon. Counsel
First vowel A – to lead   wolf.

Raoul   91633   22   Anglo-Saxon. Counsel
First vowel A – to lead   wolf.

Remus   95431   22   Latin. Fast rower.
First vowel E – to communicate

Roy   967   22   Celtic. Red haired.
First vowel O – to study

Name	Number	Total	Origins and Meanings
Rufus 93631 First vowel U – to protect		22	Latin. Red haired.
Russel 931153 First vowel U – to protect		22	Anglo-Saxon. Red as a fox.
Rusty 93127 First vowel U – to protect		22	Anglo-Saxon. Red haired.
Ryan 9715 First vowel A – to lead		22	Gaelic. Small king.
Sewell 155533 First vowel E – to communicate		22	Anglo-Saxon. Sea powerful.
Stanton 1215265 First vowel A – to lead		22	Anglo-Saxon. From the rocky wave, from the stony farm.
Stanway 1215517 First vowel A – to lead		22	Anglo-Saxon. From the stony road.
Steven 125455 First vowel E – to communicate		22	Greek. The crowned one.
Storm 12694 First vowel O – to study		22	Anglo-Saxon. The tempest.
Taffy 21667 First vowel A – to lead		22	Celtic. Welsh form of David.
Teddy 25447 First vowel E – to communicate		22	Anglo-Saxon. Prosperous guardian.
Thomas 286411 First vowel O – to study		22	Hebrew. Twin or devoted brother.
Tracy 29137 First vowel A – to lead		22	Latin. Bold and courageous.
Wallis 513391 First vowel A – to lead		22	Anglo-Saxon. The Welshman, the stranger.
Walton 513265 First vowel A – to lead		22	Anglo-Saxon. From the forest town.
Welsh 55318 First vowel E – to communicate		22	Anglo-Saxon. The Welshman.
Wynn 5755 No vowel, I sound		22	Anglo-Saxon. Dweller by a willow tree.

NUMBER 33 NAMES – GIRLS

Name	Number	Total	Origins and Meanings
Cecilia	3539391	33	Latin. Patron saint of music.
First vowel E – to communicate			
Clarice	3319935	33	French. Little shining one.
First vowel A – to lead			
Claudine	33134955	33	Latin. The lame one. Fem. of Claud.
First vowel A – to lead			
Clemence	33545535	33	Latin. Merciful and kind.
First vowel E – to communicate			
Corabella	369125331	33	Greek. Beautiful maiden.
First vowel O – to study			
Delilah	4539318	33	Hebrew. The gentle temptress.
First vowel E – to communicate			
Diahann	4918155	33	Latin (Diana). The Moon goddess.
First vowel I – intuition			
Drusilla	49319331	33	Latin. The strong one.
First vowel U – to protect			
Dagwood	4175664	33	Anglo-Saxon. Forest of the shining one.
First vowel A – to lead			
Elfreda	5369541	33	Teutonic. Elf strength.
First vowel E – to communicate			
Endocia	5546391	33	Greek. Of spotless reputation.
First vowel E – to communicate			
Esmeralda	514591341	33	French. Bright green jewel.
First vowel E – to communicate			
Giselle	7915335	33	Teutonic. A promise.
First vowel I – intuition			
Hertha	859281	33	Old English. Of the earth.
First vowel E – to communicate			
Ierne	95955	33	Latin. From Ireland.
First vowel I – intuition			
Irene	99555	33	Greek. Goddess of peace.
First vowel I – intuition			

Name	Number	Total	Origins and Meanings
Katrine First vowel A – to lead	2129955	33	Greek. Pure maiden.
Kirsten First vowel I – intuition	2991255	33	Norse. The annointed one.
Laraine First vowel A – to lead	3191955	33	Teutonic, renowned in battle, French, the queen.
Leonie First vowel E – to communicate	356595	33	Latin. The lioness.
Lexine First vowel E – to communicate	356955	33	Greek. Helper of mankind.
Lillian First vowel I – intuition	3933915	33	Latin. A lily.
Maggie First vowel A – to lead	417795	33	Latin. A pearl.
Marietta First vowel A – to lead	41995221	33	Hebrew. Bitterness.
Marylou First vowel A – to lead	4197363	33	Combination of Mary and Louise.
Mirabel First vowel I – intuition	4991253	33	Latin. Admired for her beauty.
Miranda First vowel I – intuition	4991541	33	Latin. Greatly admired.
Morgana First vowel O – to study	4697151	33	Welsh. From the seashore.
Muriel First vowel U – to protect	439953	33	Celtic. Sea bright.
Nellwyn First vowel E – to communicate	5533575	33	Greek. Friend and companion.
Nerima First vowel E – to communicate	559941	33	Greek. From the sea.
Ninette First vowel I – intuition	5955225	33	Spanish. The daughter.
Oonagh First vowel O – to study	665178	33	Latin (Una). One.
Pandora First vowel A – to lead	7154691	33	Greek. The gifted one.

Pauline	7133955	33	Latin. Little.
First vowel A – to lead			
Peggy	75777	33	Latin. A pearl (from
First vowel E – to communicate			Margaret).
Phoebe	786525	33	Greek. The bright
First vowel O – to study			shining Sun.
Poupee	763755	33	French. A doll.
First vowel O – to study			
Rosamund	96114354	33	French. Rose of the
First vowel O – to study			world.
Rufina	936951	33	Latin. Red haired one.
First vowel U – to protect			
Shelagh	1853178	33	Celtic form of Cecilia,
First vowel E – to communicate			'musical'.
Sheree	185955	33	French. Dear one.
First vowel E – to communicate			
Sheryl	185973	33	Anglo-Saxon. From the
First vowel E – to communicate			white meadow.
Villette	49335225	33	French. From the
First vowel I – intuition			village.

NUMBER 33 NAMES – BOYS

Name	Number	Total	Origins and Meanings
Allister First vowel A – to lead	13391259	33	Greek (Alexander). Helper and protector of mankind.
Beacher First vowel E – to communicate	2513859	33	Anglo-Saxon. One who lives by the oak tree.
Bishop First vowel I – intuition	291867	33	Anglo-Saxon. The bishop.
Burnard First vowel U – to protect	2395194	33	Teutonic. As brave as a bear.
Cameron First vowel A – to lead	3145965	33	Celtic. Crooked nose. Clan founder.
Cathmor First vowel A – to lead	3128469	33	Gaelic. Great warrior.
Cedric First vowel E – to communicate	354993	33	Celtic. Chieftain.
Cheney First vowel E – to communicate	385557	33	French. Oak forest dweller.
Chester First vowel E – to communicate	3851259	33	Latin. The fortified camp.
Cleveland First vowel E – to communicate	335453154	33	Anglo-Saxon. From the cliff land.
Clinton First vowel I – intuition	3395265	33	Anglo-Saxon. From the headland farm.
Cordell First vowel O – to study	3694533	33	French. The rope maker.
Cranley First vowel A – to lead	3915357	33	Anglo-Saxon. From the crane meadow.
Dagwood First vowel A – to lead	4175664	33	Anglo-Saxon. Forest of the shining one.
Dalziel First vowel A – to lead	4138953	33	Gaelic. From the little field.
Darren First vowel A – to lead	419955	33	Gaelic. Little great one.

Darryl	419973	33	French. Beloved one.
First vowel A – to lead			
Diamond	4914654	33	Anglo-Saxon. The shining protector.
First vowel I – intuition			
Erwin	59595	33	Celtic. The white river.
First vowel E – to communicate			
Fernald	6595134	33	Anglo-Saxon. From the fern slope.
First vowel E – to communicate			
Frayne	691755	33	Anglo-Saxon. A stranger.
First vowel A – to lead			
Galloway	71336517	33	Celtic. Man from the stranger Gaels.
First vowel A – to lead			
Garry	71997	33	Anglo-Saxon. Spear man.
First vowel A – to lead			
Harley	819357	33	Anglo-Saxon. From the hare meadow.
First vowel A – to lead			
Hector	853269	33	Greek. Steadfast, unswerving.
First vowel E – to communicate			
Hilton	893265	33	Anglo-Saxon. From the hill farm.
First vowel I – intuition			
Howard	865194	33	Anglo-Saxon. Chief guardian.
First vowel O – to study			
Humbert	8342592	33	Teutonic. Brilliant Hun, bright home.
First vowel U – to protect			
Ichabod	9381264	33	Hebrew. The glory has departed.
First vowel I – intuition			
Kennedy	2555547	33	Gaelic. The helmeted chief.
First vowel E – to communicate			
Knight .	259782	33	Anglo-Saxon. Mounted soldier.
First vowel I – intuition			
Leonard	3565194	33	Latin. Lion brave, courageous.
First vowel E – to communicate			
Marmaduke	419414325	33	Celtic. Sea leader.
First vowel A – to lead			
Merlyn	459375	33	Anglo-Saxon. The falcon.
First vowel E – to communicate			
Michael	4938153	33	Hebrew. Like unto the Lord.
First vowel I – intuition			

Name	Number	Total	Origins and Meanings
Millard 4933194 First vowel I – intuition		33	French. Strong and victorious.
Miller 493359 First vowel I – intuition		33	Anglo-Saxon. Grain grinder.
Montague 46521735 First vowel O – to study		33	French. From the pointed mountain.
Morven 469455 First vowel O – to study		33	Gaelic. Blond giant.
Murray 439917 First vowel U – to protect		33	Celtic. Mariner, sea fighter.
Norton 569265 First vowel O – to study		33	Anglo-Saxon. From the north farm.
Orvin 69495 First vowel O – to study		33	Anglo-Saxon. Spear friend.
Parker 719259 First vowel A – to lead		33	Anglo-Saxon. Park keeper.
Parkin 719295 First vowel A – to lead		33	Anglo-Saxon. Little Peter.
Parnell 7195533 First vowel A – to lead		33	Latin (Peter). The stone or rock.
Parry 71997 First vowel A – to lead		33	Celtic, Harry's son. French, protector.
Patrick 7129932 First vowel A – to lead		33	Latin. One of noble birth.
Philo 78936 First vowel I – intuition		33	Greek. Friendly love.
Price 79935 First vowel I – intuition		33	Celtic. Son of loving man.
Raymund 9174354 First vowel A – to lead		33	Teutonic. Wise protection.
Rhodes 986451 First vowel O – to study		33	Greek. The place of roses.
Robert 962592 First vowel O – to study		33	Teutonic. A man of brilliant reputation.
Rolph 96378 First vowel O – to study		33	Anglo-Saxon. Counsel wolf.

Roslin	961395	33	French. Small, red-haired one.
First vowel O – to study			
Rover	96459	33	Anglo-Saxon. Wanderer.
First vowel O – to study			
Rowland	9653154	33	Teutonic. From famed land.
First vowel O – to study			
Sheehan	1855815	33	Gaelic. Peaceful one.
First vowel E – to communicate			
Sherman	1859415	33	Anglo-Saxon. Wool shearer.
First vowel E – to communicate			
Sigmund	1974354	33	Teutonic. Victorious protector.
First vowel I – intuition			
Skerry	125997	33	Scandinavian. From the rocky island.
First vowel E – to communicate			
Somerset	16459152	33	Anglo-Saxon. From the summer place.
First vowel O – to study			
Sorrel	169953	33	French. With brownish hair.
First vowel O – to study			
Stamford	12146694	33	Anglo-Saxon. From the stony crossing.
First vowel A – to lead			
Stephen	1257855	33	Greek. The crowned one.
First vowel E – to communicate			
Sweeney	1555557	33	Gaelic. Little hero.
First vowel E – to communicate			
Swinton	1595265	33	Anglo-Saxon. From the pig farm.
First vowel I – intuition			
Thorald	2869134	33	Scandinavian. Thor's ruler.
First vowel O – to study			
Tormey	269457	33	Gaelic. Thunder spirit.
First vowel O – to study			
Victor	493269	33	Latin. Conqueror.
First vowel I – intuition			
Vincent	4953552	33	Latin. Conqueror.
First vowel I – intuition			
Waldron	5134965	33	Teutonic. Strength of the raven.
First vowel A – to lead			
Watford	5126694	33	Anglo-Saxon. From the hurdle by the ford.
First vowel A – to lead			

Name	Number	Total	Origins and Meanings
Wilkie First vowel I – intuition	593295	33	Teutonic. Determined protector.
Wilmur First vowel I – intuition	593439	33	Teutonic. Resolute and famous.
Winston First vowel I – intuition	5951265	33	Anglo-Saxon. From the friendly estate.
Woosley First vowel O – to study	5661357	33	Anglo-Saxon. Victorious wolf.